Involving the Community

Involving the Community

A Guide to Participatory Development Communication

Guy Bessette

SOUTHBOUND
Penang

International Development Research Centre
Ottawa · Cairo · Dakar · Montevideo · Nairobi · New Delhi · Singapore

© International Development Research Centre, 2004

Jointly published by
Southbound
Suite 20F Northam House
55 Jalan Sultan Ahmad Shah
10050 Penang, Malaysia
E-mail: books@southbound.com.my
URL: http://www.southbound.com.my
ISBN 983-9054-41-4

and the
International Development Research Centre
PO Box 8500, Ottawa, Ontario, Canada K1G 3H9
E-mail: info@idrc.ca
URL: http://www.idrc.ca
ISBN 1-55250-066-7

Note on gender

In this publication, the feminine implies the masculine in references to researchers,
practitioners and their partners in the communities in which they work.

Photographs by Guy Bessette
except for the picture on p. 131 which is by Félix Zinsou.
The figures on pp. 34,35 and 37 were rendered by Adrian Cheah.
Infography by Noémie Bessette & Lucie Brunel Design.

Typeset by Chin Kooi Hong in Baskerville 9.5/11.5 points
Cover design by Adrian Cheah, C-Square Sdn. Bhd.
Pre-press services by Eefar Lithographic Sdn. Bhd., Penang, Malaysia
Printed by Jutaprint, Penang, Malaysia.
First printing March 2004. Second printing April 2005.

Perpustakaan Negara Malaysia Cataloguing-in-Publication Data

Bessette, Guy
    Involving the community: A guide to participatory
    development communication / Guy Bessette.
    Bibliography: p.143.
    ISBN 983-9054-41-4
    1. Communication in community development. 2. Mass media
    in community development. I. Title.
    302.2

Contents

Methodology

How to plan a participatory development communication strategy

Tools

Using communication tools with a participatory approach

Foreword

Some academics write treatises about communication in development but do not undertake "projects". Most communication practitioners, on the other hand, know well the highs and lows of field implementation but do not publish.

The author of this book is an exception to both rules: a Ph.D holder who is also a practitioner who collates his experiences into a handbook to serve as a guide to others.

For those who equate communication with media, the idea the book expounds that communication is a facilitator of the development process may seem odd. This is not so for those who see development as people in communities actively and freely participating in tasks whose object is to make their collective lives better. Then communication means the interaction that must happen between and among the participants and also their environment if some common ground is to be reached by which their objective can be achieved. Hence communication virtually becomes the development process itself and the stakeholders – be they the community members or their various supporters who share an interest in the outcome – are development communicators as well.

The author uses environmental and natural resource management as the context in which to illustrate participatory development communication. However, he points out its equal utility in other development areas. He lays down its root concepts, walks the reader through a 10-step methodology for its application, and suggests some communication tools appropriate to the approach. Appended to the body of the book is a summary of the changing perception of the relationship between the twin processes of communication and development as the concept of development communication has evolved over the years. It adds a theoretical background to the material that gives it more depth not only for the development researcher and practitioner for whom the book is intended but also for development communication students who are the researchers, practitioners and policymakers of the future.

If the definition of development is communities willingly participating in the very processes that lead to it, would not "participatory" in participatory development communication be superfluous? The author wrestled with the question ... and finally decided to keep the qualifier in the book title. His decision is understandable. Until people's participation is universally accepted as the first essential to their development, then one had better continue underlining the point that the communication associated with it has to be participatory!

Nora Quebral
Los Banos

About the author

Guy Bessette is a senior program specialist for Canada's International Development Research Centre in the area of environment and natural resource management. Dr Bessette specializes in development communication and participatory development. He holds a doctorate in educational technology and has authored two other books on development communication: *Participatory Development Communication: A West African Agenda* (IDRC/Southbound 1996) and *L'appui au développement communautaire : Une expérience de communication en Afrique rurale de l'Ouest* (IDRC/L'Agence intergouvernementale de la Francophonie 2000).

Introduction

Putting people first

This is what development must be all about. But how do we achieve it in the context of poverty, and specifically in the context of natural resource management? Promoting community self-organization is the only approach when the state does not have the necessary resources to assume all of its responsibilities regarding human basic needs and socio-economic development.

Participatory development communication

Participatory development communication is a powerful tool to facilitate this process, when it accompanies local development dynamics. It is about encouraging community participation with development initiatives through a strategic utilization of various communication strategies.

By "community participation", we mean facilitating the active involvement of different community groups, together with the other stakeholders involved, and the many development and research agents working with the community and decision makers.

This guide presents its concepts and methodology. It is intended for the members of research teams, their development partners working with communities, community members involved in research or development activities and for practitioners involved in this field.

It introduces participatory development communication; addresses topics related to the use of effective two-way communication with local communities and other stakeholders; and presents a methodology to plan, develop and evaluate effective communication strategies.

How can researchers and practitioners improve communication with local communities and other stakeholders? How can two-way communication enhance community participation in research and development initiatives and improve the capacity of communities to participate in the management of their natural resources? How can researchers, community members and development practitioners improve their ability to effectively reach policy makers and promote change?

Tackling development problems, and experimenting and implementing appropriate solutions cannot be done only by researchers, extension workers and development practitioners. The process must be based on the active participation of the end users and involve the other stakeholders working with the communities. This is the fundamental basis of participatory development communication.

Traditionally, in the context of natural resource management, many communication efforts have focused on the dissemination of information and adoption of technical packages. The transfer of messages from experts to farmers, in a top-down approach however, did not yield the expected results. Rather, experience teaches us that it is much more effective to use appropriate communication strategies to build capability within local communities:

- To discuss natural resource management practices and problems;
- To identify, analyze and prioritize problems and needs;
- To identify and implement concrete initiatives to respond to those problems;
- To identify and acquire the knowledge required to implement such initiatives;
- To monitor and evaluate their efforts and plan for future action.

This communication process brings together all stakeholders – experts, farmers, extension workers, NGOs, technical services – in a dialogue and exchange of ideas on development needs, objectives and actions. It is a two-way horizontal process.

Using communication for facilitating community participation depends first and foremost on the abilities of the researchers and practitioners to strengthen the capacity of individuals and community groups in carrying out these five tasks. This guide offers an introduction to concepts and methodologies for making this process effective.

It is intended to help research teams, community groups, governmental services, and development organizations active in the field of environment and natural resource management to improve effective two-way communication with local communities and other stakeholders. It could also be useful to community media who want to strengthen their role in reinforcing local development initiatives. Finally, the guide is also meant for international agencies who support development research and initiatives in this field.

Originally intended as a reference document, it can also be used as a guide for training sessions. In fact it should be useful to anyone who is interested in the approach presented here and who wishes to adapt it to her own sector of intervention, outside the specific field of environment and natural resource management.

The methodology presented here, however, is to be considered as a starting point to the practice of participatory development communication, not as a recipe. It has to be adapted to each different context, by the main actors involved in the research or development activities.

The guide consists of three parts: Roles, Methodology and Tools.

The first part, **roles**, presents participatory development communication. It discusses the notions of development communication, development, participation and research-action, and defines the roles of research teams and practitioners in using communication to facilitate community participation.

The second part, **methodology**, introduces a methodological approach for planning communication strategies. This approach consists of ten steps: establishing a relationship with a local community; involving people in the identification of a development problem, its potential solution and an action to implement; identifying the people concerned with the problem and the action to carry out; identifying communication needs, objectives and activities; choosing communication tools; preparing and pre-testing communication content and materials; building partnership and collaboration; producing an implementation plan; planning monitoring, documentation and evaluation; planning the sharing and utilization of results.

The third part, **tools**, discusses conditions for the effective utilization of some communication tools within a participatory approach.

We invite individuals and organizations using this guide to send us their feedback and suggestions for improving future editions of the guide. Our address is indicated at the end of the publication.

Roles

The researcher or development practitioner as a communication actor

Roles

Introduction

The purpose of this first part is to introduce the principal concepts associated with participatory development communication. Specifically, it should assist you to:

1. Reflect on your role as a researcher or development practitioner interacting with local communities.

2. Identify the potential and limitations of participatory development communication for facilitating participation in research and development.

3. Identify the various dimensions involved in using participatory development communication with communities and other stakeholders.

The researcher and the development practitioner as a communication actor

Communication is an essential part of participatory research and development. As the researcher working with a community or as a development practitioner, you are first of all a communication actor. The way you approach a local community, the attitude you adopt in interacting with community members, the way you understand and discuss issues, the way you collect and share information, all involve ways of establishing communication with people.

The way communication is established and nurtured will affect how involved people will feel about the issues raised and how they will participate – or not – in a research or development initiative.

Effective communication is two-way communication; it should not be a one-way dissemination of information, nor should it consist of telling people what they should or should not do. It should not be viewed as a way to motivate people to participate in activities in which they did not have an input. The role of the researcher or development practitioner interacting with a community should consist of establishing a dialogue with community members on development issues related to its mandate, and in facilitating this dialogue between community groups.

Participatory development communication

For many people, the term "communication" still suggests the use of the media, i.e. information dissemination activities by which printed materials, radio or television programs, educational video, etc., are used to send messages. Researchers and practitioners are often less familiar with the use of communication as an empowerment tool.

Here, when we use the terminology participatory development communication, we refer to the use of communication to facilitate community participation in a development initiative. We can define it in the following way:

> Participatory development communication is a planned activity,
> based on the one hand on participatory processes, and on the other
> hand on media and interpersonal communication, which facilitates a
> dialogue among different stakeholders, around a common
> development problem or goal, with the objective of developing and
> implementing a set of activities to contribute to its solution, or its
> realization, and which supports and accompanies this initiative.

By **stakeholders**, we mean community members, active community groups, local and regional authorities, NGOs, government technical services or other institutions working at the community level, policy makers who are or should be involved with a given development initiative.

This kind of communication means moving from a focus of informing and persuading people to change their behavior or attitudes, to a focus on facilitating exchanges between different stakeholders to address a common problem. This could lead to a common development initiative to experiment with possible solutions and to identify what is needed to support the initiative in terms of partnerships, knowledge and material conditions.

The same process can be adopted when the point of departure is not a development problem but a common goal set at the community level. These exchanges also serve to articulate that goal, to lead to a set of activities to realize it and to identify what is needed in terms of partnership, knowledge, and material conditions.

The researcher and development practitioner as a facilitator

In either case, the researcher or the development practitioner uses communication as a tool to facilitate participation.

Often researchers and practitioners will adopt a vertical approach: they will identify a problem in a given community and experiment solutions with the collaboration of local people. On the communication side, the trend is to inform people of the many dimensions of that problem and of the solution they should implement and to mobilize them into action. But this way of working has little impact. After the completion of the research or the development project, things tend to return to the usual.

This reflects the old paradigm of research for development, in which the researcher applies her knowledge to the resolution of a problem, with the collaboration of a local community, and publishes her results. In the new paradigm, the researcher or development practitioner comes in as a facilitator of a process, which involves local communities and other stakeholders in the resolution of a problem or the realization of a common goal.

This requires a change of attitude. The researcher must perceive the communities not as beneficiaries but as stakeholders. You must also be ready to develop partnerships and synergy with other development actors working with the same communities.

Acting like a facilitator does not come automatically. One must learn to listen to people, to help them express their views and to assist in building consensus for action. For many researchers and development practitioners, this is a new role for which they may not have been prepared. It is a new way of doing research and development.

Making participatory research and development more effective

Participatory development communication offers another way of doing research and development projects with communities. Its methodology can be described around three sets of events:

The **first set of events** involves approaching a local community by:

- Establishing contact with a local community;
- Understanding the local setting.

The **second set of events** involves the community and other stakeholders in planning a development research or initiative. It involves bringing people to:

- Identify a given development problem or a common goal;
- Discover its many dimensions and potential solutions (in the case of a problem) or prerequisites (in the case of a goal);
- Decide on a set of actions they want to experiment with or implement;
- Identify the necessary conditions in terms of knowledge, partnership and material conditions.

That set of actions should coincide with the objectives of the research or the development project. Ideally, those should be identified at that moment. In practice, they are often identified a long time before because of the constraints of the research proposal or project presentation. When this is the case, one way to do it is to include in the proposal the review and finalization of the objectives and activities by the community as a first set of activities.

The **third set of events** consists of developing a communication strategy. It involves the following:

- Preparing and implementing a communication plan to support the set of actions identified by the stakeholders;

- Facilitating the building of partnerships;
- Facilitating the acquisition of knowledge necessary to implement these activities;
- Planning the sharing and utilization of results.

However, it is important to realize that if there is no guarantee that the necessary material conditions can be acquired, communication alone cannot be of great help.

Researchers and development practitioners involved in participatory research, where environmental and NRM problems are defined with the community, are already practicing the first steps presented here and should find it easy to integrate the other subsequent steps of PDC.

On the other hand, people involved in research or other development activities, where the problem has already been identified and the research or project design already produced, will probably find it more difficult unless they return to the community and open discussion on the a priori of the research or project.

In that kind of situation, PDC approaches will help you as researchers and practitioners to link more closely the research or project by involving the different stakeholders, thus ensuring more developmental impact.

Where does it come from?

Participatory development communication can be seen as a child of development communication and Participatory Research.

Although the term "development communication" is sometimes used to indicate the overall contribution of communication to the development of society, or sometimes to indicate the use of mass media to discuss development themes, it generally refers to the planned use of strategies and processes of communication aimed at achieving development.

It must be said that development communication is not a homogeneous field but rather a broad area in which one finds many approaches and various schools of thought and ideologies. Adult Education, Extension, IEC (information, education, communication), Advocacy, Enter-Educate (the use of entertainment to educate), and Social Marketing are some of the main approaches we find in the field.

Depending on the different methodological approaches, the definition of what development communication is will vary. However, beyond the differences in ideologies and methodological approaches, we may underscore that the lessons learned from experience in this field have demonstrated the importance of emphasizing interactive and participatory processes, rather than the production and dissemination of information apart from community processes.

The concept of development communication arose within the framework of the contribution that communication and the media made to development in the countries of the Third World. In the 1950s and 1960s, many donor agencies, such as UNESCO, USAID, the Food and Agriculture Organization (FAO), the United Nations Development Programme (UNDP) and the United Nations Children's Fund (UNICEF), sponsored numerous projects using media for communication, information or educational purposes, with a view to facilitate development, and subsequently promoted communication within the framework of development project implementation.

As for the expression "development communication", according to the Clearinghouse for Development Communication, it was apparently first used in the Philippines in the 1970s by Professor Nora Quebral to designate the processes for transmitting and communicating new knowledge related to rural environments. The field of knowledge was then extended to all those seeking to help improve the living conditions of the disadvantaged people. In the same period, Erskine Childers strongly promoted "Development Support Communication" in the UNDP system, insisting on the importance of having a communication component in all development projects.

Major trends in development communication

The experience of the past fifty years has demonstrated the crucial importance of communication in the field of development. Within this perspective of development communication, two trends developed successively: an approach that favoured large-scale actions and relied on the mass media, and an approach that promoted grassroots communication (also called community communication) via small-scale projects and use of small media (videos, posters, slide presentation, etc.).

These trends, which still co-exist today to various degrees within the field of development communication, are linked to the evolution of the development and communication models that have marked development efforts up to now. (We present those trends and the evolution in development communication in the Annex.)

The limits of participatory development communication

Because they provide support for local development initiatives, these communication activities have a direct impact on community participation in local development. Even where communication activities are relatively weak, we often find that they are useful to rally local energies around a development problem and its solutions.

Regardless of how they are conducted or what their results may be, these development communication activities encourage people to believe that their development problems are not insurmountable and that, rather than being passive onlookers, they can take action on their own.

Yet communication is not enough by itself. The development efforts that it supports also need financial and material resources and, in many cases, a degree of political will. Again, where the situation is appropriate, communication may be intended to bring together all these conditions and place them at the service of an identified development activity. Where the concrete means of implementation are lacking, or where it is not clear that they will be available, it is important to recognize that communication alone is not enough to achieve the development objectives identified.

Similarly, communication is not the answer to every development problem. There are some problems, or aspects of problems, that communication can help resolve promptly; for others, it can contribute over the longer term; while for still others it will be of little use.

Finally, participation is not a panacea or a magic wand. It is not easy to achieve and does not bring miracle results. It takes a lot of time and involvement. It can also generate frustration. Sometimes it may not be possible to achieve it. So one must be aware of those limitations, knowing at the same time that sustainable development cannot happen without it.

Implementing a participatory view of development

The first models of development were mostly defined by economic variables. It was thought that wealth, once acquired, would automatically enhance a society's well-being and living standards. At the same time, communication was considered as a process for disseminating information. For example, in the field of natural resource management, the emphasis was put on the delivery of technical packages, which were meant to provide the information and solutions people needed to address their problems.

These practices did not achieve much impact. Since then, models of development and communication have evolved considerably. We have learned to think of development as a global process, for which societies are responsible. It is not something that can be brought in from outside. Each society must define its own model of development in the light of its specific context, its culture, its resources and its values. The same is true for the various groups within a given community. People must play an active part in the process. Regarding communication, this vision of development implies that the emphasis should be put on facilitating participation.

We have also learned that development is not merely a question of economics or material goods: it also involves the notions of freedom, equitable income distribution, political openness, access to education, etc.

Participation is central to the task of defining and achieving development. But in spite of this evolution in our understanding of development, some researchers and development practitioners continue to work in a "top-down" approach. In such an approach, they are the ones who select a development problem to be tackled, identify potential solutions and develop an experimentation or implementation plan. They lead the entire process. The practice of participatory development communication should help them associate the different stakeholders in that exercise.

A further lesson is that there are limits to the ability of communication in facilitating development. First, any action is inherently limited in scope: a single series of communication activities will not change local attitudes, end desertification or invent agrarian reform overnight.

There are also limitations in terms of abilities and capacities. There are some things that communities can do by themselves, with their own resources. Then there are cases where other people must be involved, or where there are certain conditions that must be assembled. Finally, there are issues that cannot be resolved by local communities alone (e.g. policies and laws) and where they must involve other stakeholders and plan for the long term. Development practitioners and researchers must therefore help local people set realistic objectives and time frames for their action.

Development is generally not visible immediately. Yet the first step on the road to development is clear to all: it is the people's conviction that they can change things for the better, their refusal to be the permanent victims of any situation, and the emergence of a sense of self-confidence.

Development can also be characterized by the process that is implemented to attain it: strengthening a community's capacity to undertake initiatives to resolve concrete natural resource management problems, identifying and analyzing these problems, and deciding and implementing appropriate solutions. Undertaking these steps in the name of communities, but without their participation, does not lead to much impact.

Development is no longer considered as a process being directed toward beneficiaries, but as a result of the involvement and effort of people. Participation is an essential condition to this task and communication is the process that facilitates it.

Community participation

Should we continue to speak of "participation"? It has been the central development concept of the last decades and nearly everyone refers to it. Yet, in practice, it covers many "non-participatory" approaches.

For example, we cannot really refer to a participatory approach when researchers and development practitioners use participatory techniques in a context where they have already decided on the issue and where they use the information generated for the purposes of the research or development project itself, rather than for the purposes of a community-owned initiative.

The concept of "participation" is used in many ways and covers practices of all kinds. Sometimes it is used as a legitimization of non-participatory approaches. In some cases, people will say "it is participatory because we did PRA (participatory rural appraisal) with the community" when in fact they utilized a technique without an understanding of the underlying fundamentals. In fact, such techniques should help build a process where community members take ownership of a development initiative.

Participation is not limited to the notion of "consultation". In development, communities must be involved in identifying their own development problems, in seeking solutions, and in taking decisions about how to implement them. If there is some generation of information, it should be conducted in order to help the community understand and act upon the debated issues, not as an "extractive process", as has generally been the case with traditional research.

Participation does not equate mobilization either. The concept goes well beyond enlisting community support for a development project defined by authorities, NGOs or experts. This cannot lead to the expected results in a sustainable way because decisions are taken outside the community.

So what is "participation" all about? We may say that a good indicator of participation is when people take responsibility for carrying out a development initiative. This means that people are not only taking part in the different activities, but also in the

A community meeting in the Sahel. Is it consultation,mobilization or participation?
True participation is not only people gettingtogether. They must be able
to contribute to a decision-making process.

decision-making process and the planning of the development
initiative.

To facilitate participation, research teams and development
practitioners must consider the people they want to communicate
with as partners in a development effort, and not merely as
beneficiaries. The corollary on the communication side is that
efforts must be made to bring people into the discussion on the
development problem or the goal to be addressed and the actions
to be undertaken.

The concept of participation also involves that of
"community". If the goal is to facilitate participation, we must
not forget that a local community is not a unified group of people,
but rather a grouping of individuals and groups with their own
characteristics and their own interests. It often happens that
decisions taken in the name of the community in fact reflect the
interests of one group or another. At this point, communication
becomes a guise for manipulation. It is important then, to identify
clearly the different community groups that are affected by a

common development problem and who are willing and able to deal with it, and to ensure that each group can express its own viewpoint.

Participation also goes hand in hand with responsibility. It is useful here to distinguish the roles and responsibilities of the various stakeholders involved and to work out participants' material or financial contribution to the process. This contribution can take many forms: services, materials, funding, etc. However small it may be, it will help participants feel a sense of ownership over the communication activity. Without ownership, the effort will always be seen as "someone else's" initiative.

Promoting participation also depends on making room for democracy and recognizing the right to express divergent opinions. Without democracy and respect for fundamental human rights, and without the freedom of expression, the ability to use communication to foster social change is severely limited. Democracy implies recognizing other peoples' right to exist, to have their own points of view, and to express them freely, as long as they do so peacefully, without inciting hatred or bullying other people. When this ethos does not exist, participatory development communication cannot be of much help.

Obviously, recognizing the right to express divergent opinions can pose problems in many settings. Also, in many cultures, this runs counter to traditions that recognize the unarguable superiority of the Chief's opinion, or that reserve decision-making powers for the community elders. In such a setting, how are women or young people to express themselves? How can we avoid violence in situations where viewpoints or actions run counter to the will of traditional or political authorities, or set different groups against each other?

In using communication, you must be aware of all these factors: you must understand what is legally and socially accepted and acceptable, and be ready to deal with situations where the freedom of expression is suppressed or severely constrained. Thus, when development actions involve changes in the law or in the way things are done, or imply confrontation between the priviledges assigned to different groups; the situation can become delicate indeed. In these situations, researchers and practitioners are ethically bound not to provoke conflicts by their own acts, for which the participants would end up paying the price.

Using communication to facilitate participation

We have discussed the need to go beyond transmitting messages or information and persuading people. The role of the researcher or development practitioner in using communication does not consist in transmitting or disseminating messages, but in facilitating participation in local development.

The success of communication activities is closely linked to the perception of the researcher or development practitioner's role as facilitating that process of community participation. If you see your role as conceiving and disseminating messages, you will no longer be of help to community groups in identifying development problems and implementing action. Similarly, you must be careful not to substitute yourself, often unsuccessfully, for the competent local technical resources; instead you must facilitate their collaboration and participation in the development initiative identified.

As well, you must learn to involve community groups more closely in the communication strategy, and help them take ownership of the initiative rather than seeing themselves as beneficiaries of a research or development intervention.

To facilitate this participation, the researcher or development practitioner must be prepared to assume several different functions:

- Facilitate dialogue and the exchange of ideas among different groups and specific individuals: this presupposes a sound understanding of the local setting.
- Encourage thinking about local development problems and possible solutions or about a common goal to achieve the desired results: this presupposes a thorough understanding of the subject, or enlisting people who have such an understanding.
- Support the identification and realization of a concrete set of actions for experimenting or implementing the solutions identified or for achieving an identified development goal: by facilitating the different groups involved in those actions to share their views.
- Support efforts at awareness-building, motivation, learning and implementing the development action: by using communication strategies appropriate to each group of participants.
- Ensure the effective circulation of information among different participants: by using communication tools and channels appropriate to the groups involved.
- Support decision-making: by facilitating consensus among different categories of players.
- Develop local collaboration and partnerships by establishing alliances with local resource persons and agencies and serving as a conduit between the groups and these partners.
- Monitor the development initiative: by ensuring that actions taken are followed and evaluated.
- Make sure that the authorities or resource agencies in a position to assist the development action are aware of local viewpoints and needs.

Implementing such a process demands many skills including the capacity to act at different levels. The following six areas are considered to be key skill areas for researchers and development practitioners.

Developing a two-way communication process

The researcher or development practitioner must first learn to **establish a dialogue** with a community. You should be able to bring people to express their points of view and listen to others, and to build consensus around a course of action. This demands the ability to listen, to be aware of the participants' viewpoints and to be in a position to bring them to share information and views.

At the local level, in many people's minds, researchers and development practitioners are considered as a type of authority: therefore they are expected to speak and community members, with the exception of local authorities, are not used to taking part in such exchanges. This new role requires a change of attitudes.

Researchers and development practitioners should not act like schoolteachers insisting on a quiet and attentive class. Nor should they try to mobilize people in support of actions that they neither choose nor desire. Their role should be to develop a two-way communication process.

Planning and developing a communication strategy

On the basis of that two-way communication process with members of the local community, another function consists of

planning and implementing a communication strategy. This will be discussed in details in part 2 of this guide.

Facilitating learning

Where the goal of the research or the development action involves acquiring knowledge and developing skills or know-how that will allow participants to implement a development initiative of their own choosing, communication must also **facilitate the learning process**.

Adult education has demonstrated that people learn better through a non-directive teaching approach, where learning is active and takes their experience into account, as well as their knowledge and their way of seeing the world. Accordingly, you should act as facilitators of that process. It can be difficult to follow this approach if you have not been trained accordingly. At this point, research teams or practitioners may want to enlist the collaboration of a resource person who has these capacities and who can help facilitate learning and knowledge acquisition.

Moderating discussions

As a communication facilitator, you are **also a moderator**: you must listen to the various viewpoints expressed, create opportunities for interchange, encourage participants to state their views, resolve conflicts, and be judicious in the use of time available, while keeping the discussion on track.

Discussion and exchange of viewpoints should lead to decisions about how to implement the solution selected. You must therefore **be able to sum up the debate, introduce a decision-making process, and facilitate consensus**. This is not always easy: it may sometimes be necessary to expose attempts by an individual or an interest group to manipulate the decision. Since not everyone is equally endowed with such skills, it may be best in some situations to look for a moderator within the local community or to associate such a person in the research team.

Formatting and shaping information

Another function consists of **making information accessible**, in a form consistent with the characteristics of the participants in the communication process. Information on desertification prevention, for example, will not necessarily have the same meaning for nurses, peasants, soldiers, traders and youngsters. A new farming technique will not be viewed or understood in the same way by a poor, illiterate peasant and by a prosperous, educated farmer.

Encouraging and organizing women participation

Finally, it is important that women be encouraged to serve as communication facilitators. In many countries, where the agents employed by development organizations and technical extension services, or the members of research teams are mainly men, a real effort is needed to recruit female communication facilitators to take part in activities.

It will often be found that women alone are able to communicate truly with other women about their needs and to help them channel their efforts to bring about change. Indeed, in most settings, only women can approach other women, encourage them to speak their minds, and assist them in the process of individual or social change.

Participatory research and participatory development communication

Participatory development communication supports a participatory development or research for development process. It is about facilitating community participation through a strategic utilization of communication. As such, it brings together the approaches and techniques of participatory research and development with those of development communication. This implies a few important characteristics as follows:

First, within this framework, researchers, practitioners and community members learn together through joint action and reflection. It is important to state that there is no single, all-purpose recipe. Each time we must look for the best way to establish and nurture the kind of communication that will encourage and foster participation in a concrete initiative for change and support the sharing and utilization of learning.

This also means that we are allowed to make mistakes and that we learn from analyzing our successes and our failures. This is why it is important to check regularly to see that what we are doing is producing the desired results, and ask if it would be better to alter course along the way. Thus, instead of following a rigid, predetermined plan, we must be able to readjust our aim as we go along and learn from practical field experience.

Researchers and development practitioners, as well as community members and other stakeholders who are involved in the process should also be engaged in continuous monitoring and evaluation, in order to draw conclusions, apply them in practice, and then question them again. This is a continual cycle of action and reflection, through which everyone learns and improves upon their efforts.

In this first part we already mentioned some of the prerequisites that ideally should be present within communities and among practitioners. We also mentioned the need for an environment permissive of this kind of participatory approach, including democracy and the right to express divergent opinions. But it is also important to add that participation takes time: it has to become part of a culture. It is not that researchers or practitioners who approach the communities with such a framework will automatically enable participation to take place and lead to empowerment. Participation has to be learned by everyone.

Furthermore, in communities where there has been no tradition of free speech, or where there has been negative experiences resulting from free speech (political repression for example), or where there has been a history of conflicts (war or violent conflicts outside or within the community), participation will take a long time to evolve. At the same time, it is the only road that may lead to development.

Methodology

How to plan a
participatory development
communication strategy?

Methodology

Introduction

This part of the guide presents an integrated planning and action model for using participatory development communication. It includes ten steps that can assist you to plan and effectively implement a research or development process.

First, it is important to state that there is no single, all-purpose recipe to start a participatory development communication process. Each time we must look for the best way to establish the communication process among different community groups and stakeholders, and use it to facilitate and support participation in a concrete initiative or experimentation driven by a community to promote change.

It is important to adapt one's intervention to each different situation and to each specific group of participants with whom research teams or practitioners will work. This being said it is important to plan.

When it is question of using communication in the context of a development research or project, many development practitioners and researchers will want to start right away to identify the communication tools they will use (video, posters, radio) instead of planning the intervention as a whole. This practice leads to a lack of impact, since there is no way of knowing if the chosen media activity will contribute to the resolution of a development problem or to the identified goal. It also prevents participation and the involvement of community groups in the planning and implementation of communication activities.

If we want to support a participatory process, project or research identification and planning should involve representatives of the community and other stakeholders with whom the researcher or development practitioner intends to work (for example an NGO, a department of natural resources, a community radio, etc.).

Participation in the planning process is important. The model presented here derives from the first models of development communication in which planning consisted in preparing and transmitting messages suitably adapted to target groups. We saw earlier that these first models have evolved considerably and now put the accent on two-way communication and participation. Therefore, if we want participants to become fully engaged in communication and development efforts, we must adapt this methodology and undertake participatory development communication that will foster dialogue and decision-making at each stage of the development process.

We have already stressed that using PDC demands from researchers and development practitioners a change of attitude. Traditionally, the way many research teams and practitioners used to work was to identify a problem in a community and experiment solutions with the collaboration of the local people. On the communication side, the trend was to inform and create awareness both to the many dimensions of that problem and to the solution community members should implement (from an expert point of view). We discussed earlier that this practice led to little impact, but many researchers and development practitioners still work along these lines.

Working with PDC means involving the local community in identifying the development problem (or a common goal), discovering its many dimensions, identifying potential solutions (or a set of actions) and taking a decision on a concrete set of actions to experiment or implement. It is no longer the sole responsibility of the researcher or the development practitioner and their organizations.

Using communication to support a participatory development or research process also means sharing both traditional and modern knowledge related to the analysis of problems as well as the identification of potential solutions. It also involves nurturing a process in which the experimentation design or implementation plan will be developed with the active participation of the end-users. This is the process we will be planning and nurturing.

Again, the model presented here must be used as a reference only. It has to be adapted to each different context. It is a logical process based on a prior familiarity with the local setting, begins with the expression of development needs in a given community, and involves specific stakeholders in addressing those issues, while supporting and accompanying this process of participation.

The methodological approach

Participatory development communication supports a participatory development or research for development process. We usually represent such a process through four main phases, which of course are not separated but are interlinked: diagnosis, planning, intervention or experimentation, and assessment (see Figure 1). Upon completing these phases we need to decide whether to return to the beginning of the process (diagnosis) and start another cycle; or iterate to a revision of the planning phase; or proceed with scaling-up, starting another planning, implementation and evaluation cycle.

The PDC model (see Figure 2) supports such a process with ten specific steps. The process of planning and developing PDC itself is however not sequential.

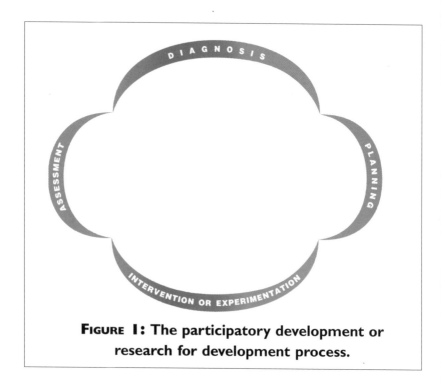

FIGURE 1: The participatory development or research for development process.

We can view those steps around a circle. This circle represents the process of facilitating participation through communication. It develops throughout the total process, during the interactions of researchers and development practitioners with the community. Moreover, all these specific steps are not primarily about applying techniques, but also about building mutual understanding and collaboration, facilitating participation and accompanying a development dynamic.

We can then place the steps of the PDC methodology on the perimeter of that circle because they all contribute to facilitating participation to the participatory development or research for development process (see Figure 3). Some of these steps can be done in parallel or in a different order. They can also be defined differently depending on the context. It is a continual process and not a linear one.

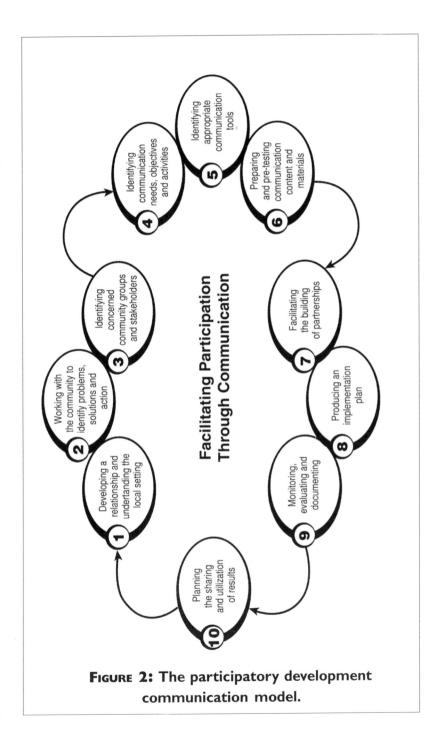

Figure 2: The participatory development communication model.

Hence it is important to consider these steps as reference points in a global and systematic process. With this reserve in mind, here are the ten different steps we usually go through to plan and implement participatory development communication:

Step 1:   Establishing a relationship with a local community and understanding the local setting

Step 2:   Involving the community in the identification of a problem, its potential solutions, and the decision to carry out a concrete initiative

Step 3:   Identifying the different community groups and other stakeholders concerned with the identified problem (or goal) and initiative

Step 4:   Identifying communication needs, objectives and activities

Step 5:   Identifying appropriate communication tools

Step 6:   Preparing and pre-testing communication content and materials

Step 7:   Facilitating partnerships

Step 8:   Producing an implementation plan

Step 9:   Monitoring and evaluating the communication strategy and documenting the development or research process

Step 10: Planning the sharing and utilization of results

Step 1: Establishing a relationship with a local community and understanding the local setting

Establishing a relationship with a local community is a process that will develop all along the way, through the interaction of research teams or development practitioners with people of that community.

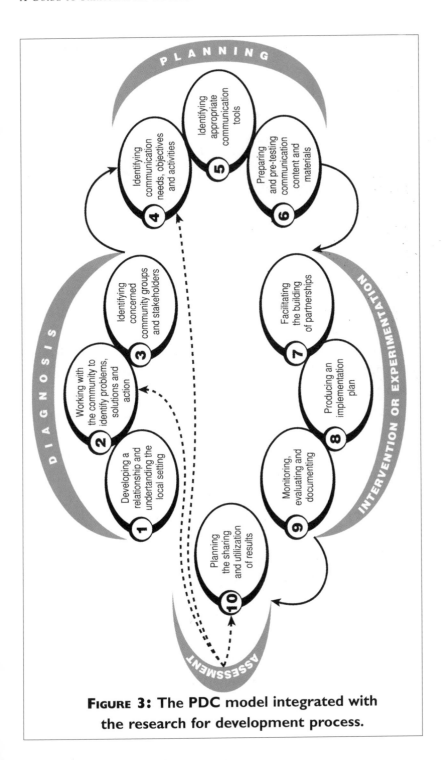

FIGURE 3: The PDC model integrated with the research for development process.

Building relationships between researchers, practitioners and community members is essential to involve people in participatory processes of research or development.

At the beginning, it refers to collecting preliminary information on the community and its environment, entering the community, getting to know the people and the resource persons in the community, developing a more thorough collection of information with the participation of the local people and resource persons, and facilitating a dialogue with them.

But what it really means is building a relationship, developing collaboration mechanisms, facilitating and nurturing the exchange of information and knowledge, negotiating roles and responsibilities, and most importantly, building mutual trust.

We will discuss the tasks involved here separately but of course, they are not sequential and overlap with one another.

Consulting existing information and planning the approach of a local community

Generally, it is researchers or development practitioners who approach a community; the other way round also happens but not very frequently. So in the first situation, there is a process of selection and there is a preliminary collection of information to support this process.

Choosing a particular community to work with

How does one choose a particular community or specific communities to work with? There are many considerations. Often, researchers will target specific communities because they are representatives of certain characteristics important for the research. Development practitioners will often target a community where they feel the need for intervention is more acute. Both will take into account opportunities for resources or travel to the field. There can be many reasons. Two of them merit special attention.

One important factor to consider is the agreement of a community to work with a research or development initiative. In many cases, the authorities of a specific community will give their agreement without the community itself being aware of this, and without understanding the implications in terms of participation and involvement in a concrete development action. This often leads to artificial situations. So before selecting a specific community to work with, it is better to discuss this in the field with different community groups and resource people, and explore the interest and potential of such work.

A second factor to consider is the link between working with a specific local community and the possibility of extending results either to other communities, or to the policy environment. This can also play an important role in the selection process.

Consulting existing information

Let us also mention that in many contexts, statistics and other information from secondary sources are not accurate. So visiting resource persons knowledgeable of the community setting or of the problem involved should complement and supplement the information. The selection itself should only be finalized after contacting and discussing with community members.

BEFORE GOING TO THE FIELD

Researchers and practitioners should develop a prior understanding of the local setting before going to the field and conducting formal meetings with a given community. Without such prior knowledge, it is often very difficult to build a sound understanding of the setting, even by conducting participatory rural appraisal activities.

This being said, it is often difficult to assemble all this knowledge. Doing so requires time and money (if only to cover travel and accommodation costs), and may demand skills that not everyone possesses. As a result, activities are often based on an incomplete understanding of the setting in which the researcher or the practitioner is trying to act, and of the problems she is trying to address. Research teams and development organizations must be aware of this and should plan time and necessary resources to understand the setting more thoroughly.

Hence the identification of relevant sources of documentation and resource people and/or organizations that know the community very well should be the first item to be considered.

In addition, when several communities are involved, the manner, order and time necessary in approaching them must also be considered. The schedule should be established taking into consideration the working and seasonal calenders of the different communities. The difficulties of access to some communities, especially during the rainy season, should also be considered, since they will have a direct effect on the amount of time researchers and practitioners will have at their disposal to work with the communities.

INTRODUCING THE RESEARCH OR DEVELOPMENT INITIATIVE TO THE COMMUNITY

Attitudes should also be given proper attention: it is not the same thing to identify three or four different field sites where a research team will work and establish a working relationship with a certain number of communities.

How will the research or development initiative be introduced to the community? Usually, the process begins with researchers or development practitioners having a set of preliminary planning meetings with the local leaders. A first visit will present the research or development initiative idea to the community leaders and ask for an agreement to discuss the idea and work with the community. Often, another visit to the community leaders will be useful to review the research or development initiative proposal before introducing it to the community.

All this takes time and should be given careful consideration. Often, this phase of the research or development initiative does not receive the attention and time it deserves.

Conducting a visit to the authorities

In many settings, a visit to the authorities in the community is part of what is required in order to enter the community. It is often important to visit both political authorities and traditional authorities, in order to inform them of the research or initiative, ask for their cooperation, and understand their perspective on what is being initiated. This should be done modestly and respectfully and is often better achieved with the help of someone from the community making the introductions.

The role of the researcher or development practitioner

As discussed earlier, in the context of participatory development communication, we must see ourselves as communication actors and realize that our way of interacting with others will influence the way people will or will not participate in the research or development initiative. In that perspective, it is important to facilitate a two-way mode of approach: the research team or development workers approaching a community through community leaders and community groups, and the community approaching the research team/development workers. The intention of establishing a dialogue should prevail over the demand for collaboration.

Attitudes and perceptions

Many researchers and development practitioners have been trained to perceive community members as beneficiaries and as future end users of the research results. A shift of perception at that level is also desirable. We have to recognize that the delivery of technologies to end users (like farmers and other community dwellers) simply does not work. A first desirable change is to consider community members as stakeholders in the development process, not as beneficiaries. So approaching a community also means involving people and thinking in terms of stakeholders' participation in the different phases of the research process as a whole.

Discussing agendas

It is important at this stage to recognize that the interests of communities, researchers and development practitioners are not similar. Generally, researchers and development practitioners come to a community with a specific mandate. So, if we want to start from the needs and priorities of the communities, it can only be done within a specific category of needs. This has to be clarified at the first moment of approaching a community. When resource people come from the outside into a poor community, people will present them with all their problems. They will not make a distinction between different categories, such as soil fertility, health, and credit facilities problems because it is all part of the same reality for them. Because you cannot address all of those issues, the scope and limitations of your mandate must be fully explained and discussed with community members.

Avoiding the danger of raising expectations

In so doing, researchers and development practitioners must be aware of the danger of raising expectations in local communities. To counteract this risk, it is important to be clear on your mandate with community members, to discuss possible negative and positive outcomes of what they will be doing together, and to involve community members in activity planning.

Talking about short-term and medium-term impact may also be useful. Some communities lose interest in a given project when they do not see any concrete "benefits" coming from it.

Finally, there is the issue of financial and material advantages for participating in research or development activities. First, we should try to find substitutes for the word "project". Whenever researchers or practitioners come to a community to discuss a "project", many people tend to see an opportunity of great sums of money and material advantages. These considerations should be addressed at the beginning of the relation with the community.

Agreement should also be made to recognize whenever compensation is justified and what form it should take. It is important here for research teams and development practitioners to be clear on this issue in order not to raise the financial expectations of community members.

Understanding culture

Among the problems that researchers and development practitioners may face in the course of their work are cultural barriers and systems of beliefs.

Cultural and religious characteristics, and the ways people approach and discuss subjects or take decisions, can vary greatly from one region to another, especially when it comes to specific social groups (women and children, for example) or ethnic groups. It is very important that you identify these cultural elements for each specific group involved in the development of the research process. Once again, it takes time to understand and appreciate these factors, in a context where there is usually little time available.

Resistance to change and the force of local customs, habits and taboos are other cultural aspects that can often pose significant obstacles. It is essential to understand and appreciate their real influence. Here again, we cannot overestimate the importance of taking sufficient time to know the community and discuss with people.

Some teams try to have some of their staff spend more time living in the communities among local farmers and organizing and participating in social activities in the communities. This can make a big difference for the outsiders in understanding the community and for the community to understand and know better those researchers or development practitioners. Visiting the village elders and collecting information from different groups are also good practices.

It is not always possible for research teams and development practitioners to do so however, as often it was not planned at the beginning of the project. This should be given better consideration.

Using local language

Language barriers are another difficulty. The use of a local interpreter can help, but a local moderator may also be needed to facilitate group discussions in the local language.

There is also the issue of the level of language. The way a topic is dealt with, the vocabulary used, the ways different groups and individuals perceive a topic will differ from one place to the next and from one group to another.

Taking time into consideration

Participation demands not only a change of attitudes from researchers and development practitioners, but also from community members. In order for people to participate meningfully in the development process, they must first develop the perception that they can make a difference, moving from a passive attitude of waiting for donors to an attitude of self-help. This takes time and does not happen in a matter of days or weeks.

Apart from attitudes, participation also demands that community members develop confidence and skills that help them participate meaningfully and effectively in research or development initiatives. Time, again.

Finally, in some contexts, community members are strongly influenced by market trends and self-interest comes before community interests. This is often linked to a breakdown of traditional systems and beliefs, in which individuals seek to use the resources as fast as possible to gain better income. So, for improvement to take place, people need to start working together again as a community. This also takes time.

Therefore, expectations regarding the achievement of research or development objectives should be tempered, taking into consideration these factors.

Understanding the local setting

As we saw, understanding the local setting goes hand in hand with the process of entering a community. But there are also some specific considerations to take into account. Facilitating communication and community participation first depends on a thorough understanding of the local setting in which the researcher or development practitioner wants to work. This also includes gathering information and knowledge related to the problem corresponding to the specific mandate of the researcher or the development practitioner.

Traditionally, communication was about whether people understood the message. But the focus should be recast the other way: how well does the researcher or practitioner understand the setting in which she is planning to work and the people she wants to work with?

This process of understanding involves the following aspects that we will now discuss.

Entering a flow

Any intervention happens in a temporal dimension. So it is important for the researcher or the development practitioner to understand that her action is connected in a certain way with a given context of past and present development initiatives.

Those initiatives may be past or present projects lead by NGOs or international organizations, but they can also be local initiatives developed by community groups and organizations. The knowledge of these interventions and of the other actors involved in these will be very useful, not only to develop potential synergies but also to understand the attitudes of community members and other stakeholders toward the "new" initiative.

Collecting and sharing information

Classical research tends to be extractive. Researchers have been trained in doing data collection at the beginning of a research initiative. Similarly, many development practitioners have been trained to collect information to feed into the design of a project.

Researchers and development practitioners working with a participatory development communication approach should try to collect and share information together with community members and associated stakeholders. The idea is to associate them to the different phases of the research or project so that researchers or development practitioners are not only receiving information from community members, but are also building a process with them.

In sharing the information they have on a local setting or development problem, researchers confirm if they understood correctly the information provided by the local people, and the people obtain a broader perspective of their community through the information that has been put together. This broader perspective also helps in involving people in the identification of a problem or a common goal, the analysis of the causes, and the decision-making on an initiative to be carried out.

Using PRA and related techniques

Many researchers and practitioners now use participatory techniques, such as participatory rural appraisal, to actively involve members of a community in quickly gathering the maximum amount of information on the state and management of natural resources, and basic social, economic and political data.

The exercises can include the use of different techniques like collective mapping of the local area, developing a time line, ranking the importance of problems inside a matrix, wealth ranking, doing observation walks, using Venn diagrams, producing seasonability diagrams, etc.

The use of PRA as a collection of techniques for putting together this information in a limited time, is a powerful tool for facilitating the participation of community members. But it can also be used restrictively, when the techniques are not fully appropriated by the participants and remain techniques used by the research team only to gather information for their own purposes.

The main idea in using PRA is to collect information quickly with the participation of community members and to share it so that everyone becomes empowered by that information and can participate better in the analysis and decision-making processes. When this does not happen, and when researchers or development practitioners go back with the information without nurturing this empowerment process, the technique is not applied as it should. In fact, such a process can be detrimental because researchers and practitioners then think that they are doing participatory work, when in fact, community members are only "being participated".

A general knowledge of the local setting

Knowledge of the local setting includes knowledge in terms of natural resource mapping and natural resource management practices, but it should go beyond that. It refers to general knowledge on the community and its environment: not just geographical, environmental and ecological, but also demographic, linguistic, religious, cultural, political, economic, social, educational issues, livelihoods and aspirations, and others.

Particularly, we will want to be able to answer the following questions:

- What is the history of that local community?
- Who are the different groups composing it and what are the main characteristics of those groups and of the relations between them?
- What is its social, political and administrative organization?
- How does this local community relate to the different orders of authority at the local, regional and national level?
- What are the major power relations and existing or latent conflicts in the community?
- What are the main socio-economic activities?
- What about health and education?
- What are the main development problems and the main development initiatives?
- What are the main customs and beliefs regarding the research team or practitioner's topic of interest, etc.

Collecting information on communication issues

In this preliminary phase of the research or development initiative, efforts should also be made to identify the different specific groups in the community. It is important not to consider community members as a homogeneous group. It is better, after an initial community meeting, to plan specific meetings with different community groups or members and ask for their own specific perspective.

Also, in the same way that they collect general information and do some PRA activities to gather more specific information, researchers and development practitioners should also ask some communication questions which will help them in a later stage to design a communication strategy. The following information will be very useful:

- How could we identify and describe the different groups composing the local community?
- What are the main characteristics of these groups and the state of the relations between them?
- What are the main customs and beliefs concerning the management of land and water (or other topic associated with the research or development intervention)?
- What are the effective interpersonal channels of communication (views expressed by opinion leaders or exchanged by people in specific places) and the institutional channels (local associations or institutions which play an important role in circulating information) that are used locally by people to exchange information and points of views?
- What modern and traditional media are utilized in the community?

As we shall see further on, all the above information will feed into the communication plan.

Developing strategies to identify reliable information

Many community members, approached in the process of collecting information, especially poor farmers, will not speak their mind in response to the questions they are being asked, but say what they think the researcher or development practitioner wants to hear. So validating the information and also developing strategies adapted to specific groups are especially useful. For example, there may be more chances in getting reliable information through a discussion with poor farmers led by a farmer rather than by an impressive outsider from the city.

Developing collaboration and partnership

These first stages of approaching a community and collecting and sharing information are also a first opportunity to identify resource persons and organizations working in the same area and to involve them in the process. It can be an NGO working with the same community, a rural radio or a theatre group, etc. It is always better to do so in the beginning, where people feel they can play a role in the design of the research or intervention than after, when they perceive themselves as mere contract providers.

Building trust

To close this part of the discussion, we must stress the importance of building trust and understanding between the researcher or development practitioner and community members.

During the implementation stage, it will also be important to maintain the motivation and interest of the participants. We cannot expect this to happen by itself without support. Participatory research or development activities will often be launched in a rush of enthusiasm, yet we must be aware that this is only one phase of a long and complex process that demands sustained attention and dedication. It is essential to be prepared to reinforce this climate of confidence and share the activity's objectives among all participants.

In that sense, the preliminary gathering of information is a way for you to start developing a dialogue with the community and involving local people and resource persons in the process.

Step 2: Involving the community in the identification of a problem, its potential solutions, and the decision to carry out a concrete initiative

A second step consists of involving the community in the identification of a problem and potential solutions, and in making a decision to carry out a concrete initiative. This means that as a facilitator of the participatory process you will help community and other stakeholders to:

- Identify a specific development problem, discuss its many dimensions, its causes and potential solutions;

OR

- A common goal that the community identifies for itself and the prerequisites or essential conditions to reach it;
- Identify a concrete initiative or set of actions that the community wants to experiment or realize;
- Identify the necessary conditions in terms of knowledge, partnership and material conditions (assess the feasibility);
- Take a decision to carry out the initiative.

That set of actions should coincide with the objectives of the research or of the development project. Ideally, those should be identified at that moment. In practice, they are often identified long before, because of the constraints of research proposal or project presentation. When this is the case, one way to do it is to include in the proposal the review and finalization of the objectives and activities by the community as a first set of activities. Where do we begin? There are several possible points of departure:

Deciding on a concrete initiative to be carried out: in this community meeting, people are not only gathered to hear useful information from resource persons, they are discussing their problems, what causes them and potential solutions. Researchers and development practitioners support and facilitate such a process, which will lead to a decision to carry out or experiment with a concrete set of activities.

Starting with a problem

The most common situation is when the research team or the practitioner seeks to work with a local community facing specific natural resource management problems.

In this context, the methodology mainly consists of implementing a process that will allow the different community groups to:

- Discuss the problems affecting their community and prioritize a specific problem;
- Identify and analyze the causes and consequences of that problem with the help of a specialist in the area of the question;
- Decide if they can act on that problem;
- Identify potential solutions with the help of a specialist;

- Decide on experimenting a set of potential solutions in particular;
- Define a communication strategy that will support the experimentation or implementation.

Facilitating synergy

Another situation is where an action has already been undertaken within a local community to deal with a natural resource management problem, either by a support agency, a development organization, a technical service or by a local group.

In this case, when it is possible, you should try to support that community initiative, instead of coming up with something different. You can facilitate the discussion on the causes of the identified problem and on potential solutions and help define the communication strategy, which will support the experimentation or the implementation.

Sometimes, a problem that many communities face with research or development initiatives is their multiplicity, often in the same areas. They are then faced with a fragmentation of activities funded by different donors and undertaken by different organizations. Synergy between those different initiatives should be pursued very seriously. It may not always be possible to do so but we can observe, in the cases where it has been done, the many benefits that result from this approach.

Starting with a goal

There is also a third situation, where the point of departure is a common goal that a community has set. Instead of focusing on what goes wrong, this approach focuses on a vision of where a community (or individuals, or community groups) wants to arrive at in a given period of time. Sometimes it will also be the case of a successful initiative that a given community group wants to share with others.

As with the process developing from problem identification where a community identifies a set of potential solutions to experiment with, in this case the community will decide on implementing a set of actions to approach that goal.

Therefore whether the process derives from a problem or from a common goal, there is a community decision to act. Ideally, this is where the research objectives or the development initiative objectives should come into play.

Putting the community first

In any of these three contexts, it should be the local people, not the research team or the development practitioner, who identify the problem to be addressed or the initiative to be carried on. The global idea is to start from people's own perceptions of their needs, rather than coming in with a preconceived project and trying to fit it in a local community. The role of the research team or development practitioner consists in facilitating this process, not in taking it on herself.

Prioritizing a development problem

When you as the researcher or development practitioner begin a new dynamic with a community, you must be clear on your mandate. As we mentioned earlier, it has to be clarified at the first moment of approaching a community. When resource people come from the outside into a poor community, people will present them with all their problems. They will not make the distinction between different categories, such as soil fertility, health and credit facilities problems because it is all part of the same reality for them. But the researcher or development practitioner cannot address all of these issues, so the scope and limitations of her mandate must be fully explained and discussed with community members.

Another dimension related to this issue is to be attentive to the power relations in the community, which will affect the prioritization. Sometimes, a development problem identified by a community can reflect the priority of an influential person of that community only (a chief, a religious leader, an opinion leader, etc.). It is important at that level to use a democratic mechanism to ensure the process remains truly participatory.

Discussing the causes of a development problem

If communication is to contribute to the resolution of a development problem, the process should bring people to understand the **causes**, identify possible **solutions** and decide what **action** to take.

There is often a temptation to jump directly from the desired goal (for example, resolving a conflict) to an action (for example, an awareness campaign) without looking closely at the underlying causes of the problem (for example, the lack of an adequate quantity of a given natural resource for all local inhabitants).

The technique of the problem tree, practiced by many NGOs, may help a group to identify a problem more clearly. The trunk of the tree represents the problem itself, and the branches, the consequences. But we must also discover the roots, which of course are hidden. This involves a lot of discussions and negotiations on what is a cause and what is a consequence. In many cases, it helps to take note of the complexity of a given problem.

For example, community members may have identified the lack of drinkable water as a major problem and may want to launch a campaign to build a well. Yet further investigation may show that there already exist some wells in the area but that they were not cared for and are no longer functional. With a little research, it may be found that the community was never associated with the project of having a well and that before digging another one, there should be some discussion on the project, the locating of the well within the locality, responsibilities for maintenance and the rights of specific community groups to drinkable water. This is where participatory development communication is particularly useful.

Again, the local people may identify desertification as a major threat to the community because soil productivity is declining and the environment is getting poorer in trees. If we go no further than this, we might be tempted to conclude that what is needed is a broad public information campaign. Yet if we document the situation, and discuss it with technical partners working in the area, we may find that some groups in the community are particularly at risk. The problem in this case is to discover how to reach these specific groups and discuss with them ways to improve their agricultural production and their livelihood.

Involving specialists

Understanding the cause of a problem often requires not only common knowledge, available locally, but also specialized knowledge. It can be someone from the community holding appropriate local knowledge, or an external specialist contributing with modern knowledge. The recourse to a specialist in discussing the causes and consequences of a given problem and in identifying its potential solutions is quite important: this is where specialized knowledge comes into play. Many problems and questions related to soil fertility or to water for example are so complex that a deficit in information at that level can lead to bad decisions.

In the case of a development intervention, it is important to get the assistance of a specialist. In the case of a research intervention, members of the research team may have specialized knowledge, but it is not always adapted to the local context. Validation of that knowledge in the local context is then an important process.

Increasing the accuracy of information in a discussion and facilitating its sharing and understanding is an important issue in the process of involving the community in the assessment of problems and solutions and should be given proper attention.

Deciding on a concrete initiative to undertake

Once the development problem and its causes have been identified, the next step is for the community to decide if they can act on that problem. As noted earlier, there are some things that communities can do by themselves, with their own resources; then there are cases where other people must be involved, or where there are certain conditions that must first be assembled. Finally, there are things that local communities cannot control directly (policies and laws, for example) and which necessitate the implementation of a complex decision-making influencing process.

If there is little possibility of implementation, then we must go back to prioritization. If there is, the next tasks are to identify potential solutions with the help of a specialist and then decide on experimenting with a set of potential solutions in particular or on implementing a specific set of activities (in the case of a goal-oriented process).

Again, in identifying possible solutions and actions to undertake, it is important to bear in mind the real constraints associated with this enterprise and to keep objectives realistic and modest.

This is where ideally, development and research objectives should be identified to strengthen and accompany the community initiative. In general, however, such objectives have already been identified in the proposal before going to such a process with the community. A way to go around this problem is to plan a revision of the initial objectives with the community at the start of the research or development project.

Adjusting choices in mid-course

In the course of an experimentation or implementation, we may need to revise the initial choices. As work proceeds, we may find that the action identified at the outset is not appropriate to the problem at hand. A problem of water access in a community may in fact turn out to be a problem of management or community participation. A project aiming to fight bush fires may first demand an initiative on soil fertility. These kinds of situations happen all the time.

In other cases, we may discover that some preliminary actions need to be taken before we can proceed with the project as planned. For example, a set of actions initially planned with women may have to wait till the realization of preliminary communication activities with their husbands or in certain cases, with the traditional authorities.

Often we will have to reassess the scope of the initial ambitions in the light of the constraints that now exist. Often too the number of activities planned must be reduced in order to take into account the time factor for their realization or the availability of the participating groups.

In any case, it is important to adopt an iterative approach and to readjust initial choices as we go on in order to better attain our objective. Going with a plan and not proceeding with any modifications on the way may be a good attitude if you are building a bridge but with human situations, it is totally different.

STEP 3: Identifying the different community groups and other stakeholders concerned with the identified problem (or goal) and initiative

Who are the different community groups and the other stakeholders concerned with the selected problem and solution?

At this stage, the research team or the development practitioner needs to identify the different community groups or categories of people concerned with a given problem or with a given development action, and to identify the best way of making contact and establishing dialogue with each of them. The same applies to the other stakeholders involved in the given problem and solution to experiment.

Addressing ourselves to a general audience such as "the community" or "the people of such-and-such village" does not really help in involving people in communication. Every group that makes up the community, in terms of age, sex, ethnic origin, language, occupation, social and economic conditions, has its own characteristics, its own way of seeing a problem and its solution, and its own way of taking actions.

In participatory development communication, the communication is targeted in order to reach specific groups. We often speak of "target population" or "target groups" to designate those to whom the communication is to be addressed. This term, of military origin, once referred to the kind of communication where the communication facilitator sought to prepare and transmit messages to reach specific groups within a given population. While we take a different approach today, where community groups are invited to become participants in the

Approaching specific groups in the community: addressing ourselves to a general audience such as "the community" or "the farmers" does not help in involving people of different groups. Every community group has it's own way of seeing a problem and its potential solutions, and its own way of taking action.

communication process, the former term still remains in use. However the metaphor is misleading and it is important to change the way we refer to the specific groups with whom we are working, if we want to modify our way of establishing a relation with them.

How do we differentiate these groups?

The main criterion for identifying the different groups is to identify the various categories of persons who are most affected by the development problem and those groups that might be able to contribute to its solution. The principle is the same if we are speaking of a development initiative rather than a problem: we must identify the people most concerned about it.

We may distinguish among these categories on the basis of factors: age, gender, language, ethnic or other specific social

*Approaching specific groups in the community: this is also true of
men and women within each of these groups.*

factors, livelihood or socio-professional categories (and periods
of availability), income, educational level, localization, culture,
values or religion, behavior or common interests.

For example, in the case of forest management, concerned
groups can include not only "youth", "women" or workers from
a logging company, but may also include a group of people who
protect a sacred area of the forest, another group consisting of
traditional pharmacologists, a group of people living on the edge
of the forest and who "clean" the forest by collecting dead fire
wood, a group collecting wood for charcoal making, etc.

Groups of participants can often be identified at the outset of
an intervention. But it may sometimes be necessary, once the
intervention is underway, to refocus or revise our initial selection
and identify the groups most specifically affected by the problem.

Similarly, we might identify other stakeholders who, although
not directly affected, have the capacity to provide assistance in
resolving the problem or in conducting the planned activities.
In the example discussed above, we might, depending on the
circumstances, call upon the assistance of traditional or religious
authorities, personalities who wield influence among the young,

such as sports heroes or popular singers, teachers or social workers.

Who and with whom?

One way to identify those specific groups is to ask first "Who is involved in the problem or in the initiative to carry out" and then ask ourselves "With whom are we going to work?"

A first list can be made out of three global categories: community groups, policy makers and other stakeholders. We then identify every group in each of these categories who is affected by the problem or can play a role in the solution. In a second list the research team or development practitioner will identify within these groups those with whom they will work as a priority.

If all the small-scale farmers of a specific county are involved with a soil fertility problem for example, the researchers or practitioners may decide to work in priority with farmers involved in actions aiming to manage the erosion, with women groups, and with poor farmers.

Similarly, although all the local and district leaders should be involved, they might concentrate their action on sub-county authorities. Within the third category, they might decide to work first with the extension people working in the area, although there are other stakeholders involved. It is a question of priorities and resources.

The gender issue: paying particular attention to the different needs and social roles of men and women

In all cases it is important to pay particular attention to the issue of gender. In every setting, the needs, social roles and responsibilities of men and women are different. The degree of

access to resources and of participation in the decision-makin
processes may also be different between men and women. A
the way they will view a common problem or potential sol·
is also very different.

The same is true for the young people of each sex
often a sharp distinction between the roles and nr
and of older women, or between older men and you..... ͜   ͜ ͜e's
perceptions of the same problem.

Consequently, their interests are different, their needs are
different, the way they see things are different, and their
contributions to development are different. Formerly, the focus
of interest was on "the community", without really taking this
difference into account. As a result, women and young people
alike were often overlooked in the development process, although
their participation was an essential condition. If their involvement
was to be enhanced, it was quickly realized that it was not enough
simply to focus on women or on young people as a separate
group: what was needed in all cases was to pay attention to the
different roles of men and women in the development situation
concerned, and to the various relationships between these roles.
It is this realization that underlies the preoccupation with gender.

From the communication perspective, the gender issue implies
two things. First, it is important to distinguish clearly between
the needs of men and women. In order to achieve this, we must
learn how to establish communication, in all settings, with both
men and women.

In many settings, women are often barred from village
meetings, or if they are admitted, they do not always have the
right to speak. Even where this inhibition is cultural rather than
formal, it must be taken into account. It often happens that
women who are authorized to participate in these meetings are
not really representative of local women as a whole. It is
important then to be aware of these realities. Within each category

Social and economic roles of men and women are different.
Needs and responsibilities also differ. This is also true of the degree of access
to resources and of participation in the decision-making processes.

of participant groups, we need to think about the specific roles
and needs of men and women.

Secondly, it is important to encourage and promote women's
participation. The challenge here is to bring women to participate
in defining problems that concern them and in seeking solutions,
rather than "mobilizing" them. Here again, depending on habits
and customs in each setting, the ways of establishing
communication will be different. Sometimes it may be necessary
to interact with the men first, and proceed only later to bring
together groups of women and discuss issues with them.

A third important aspect of the gender issue is to distinguish
between gender roles in each of the specific groups we intend to
work with and not to build separate categories of "women" and
"young people". Many researchers and development practitioners
at this stage will have the tendency to identify groups such as:
farmers, foresters, fishermen, women, young people, etc. that is
a mix of gender and socio-professional roles. But this

categorization is not very productive: first, there are women and young people in each of these socio-professional categories and their roles, needs and perceptions are often different from those of the men. Second, one has to ask how people, in each of these categories, are affected by the problem or involved in the initiative.

How well do we know each specific group?

Each specific group has its own characteristics and these must be taken into account in any communication action. In the same way, each group will be concerned with a given development problem in different ways.

For this reason, we cannot approach each group in the same manner. Moreover, each group has its own social codes and ways of doing things. Similarly, their ways of participating in communication will be different and certain conditions will have to be assembled if real communication is to be established with each group. It is important then to take the time to become familiar with each group and identify the general characteristics that must be taken into account in communication, as well as the factors that may condition their participation.

It can be useful here to draw up a profile of each group as if we were trying to describe the group to an outsider. This profile should specify:

- Physical characteristics: age, sex, etc.
- Ethnic and geographic background.
- Language and habits of communication.
- Socio-economic characteristics: lifestyle, income, education, literacy, etc.
- Cultural characteristics: traditions, values, beliefs, etc.

- Knowledge, attitudes and behaviour with respect to the development problem to be dealt with through communication.

It is also important to identify each group's own methods and channels of communication (the ways in which people interact, or specific places where they do so), not only in order to make contact initially but also to facilitate the expression of the group's viewpoints.

Finally, we need to identify the particular context of each group: the season or the time of day when its members are available, the seasonal nature of their economic occupations, their physical setting (meeting places, availability of electricity, means of communication, etc.). In fact, many communication initiatives run into difficulty because they fail to take into account this aspect.

This information-gathering process does not require an in-depth sociological survey, but rather a quick review of basic information that will serve to orient the communication strategy. This review is best done when it involves directly the representatives of the local community.

Step 4: Identifying communication needs, objectives and activities

Starting with communication needs

When planning communication strategies, many tend to take a very broad problem as a starting point (desertification, for example), and then to move right into planning communication activities (information sessions, awareness campaigns).

The result is that the target is often missed and, despite all the activities undertaken, the problem remains untouched. To avoid situations of this kind, we should start from the needs expressed by local communities and identify the communication objectives we want to achieve before undertaking specific activities.

Material needs and communication needs

Development needs can be categorized broadly between material needs and communication needs. Any given development problem and attempt to resolve it will present needs relating to material resources and to the conditions to acquire and manage these. However, we will also find complementary needs which involve communication: for sharing information, influencing policies, mediating conflicts, raising awareness, facilitating learning, supporting decision-making and collaborative action etc. Clearly, these two aspects should go hand in hand and be addressed in a systemic way by any research or development effort.

Participatory development communication puts the focus on the second category of needs and ensures that they are addressed, together with the material needs the research or development effort is concentrating on.

For example, in an initiative aiming to resolve water conflicts in a village, we will probably find a need for an improved access to water, and development initiatives are needed to address that need. At the same time however, we may find out that in order to find adequate solutions in the present context, we must first understand the reasons behind the conflicts, such as the time schedule for various categories of users or the conflicting needs of herders, women and farmers. Or we may find that villagers do not know how to set up or manage effectively a water management committee. Or there may be a need for the village authorities to advocate for more water access, such as the drilling

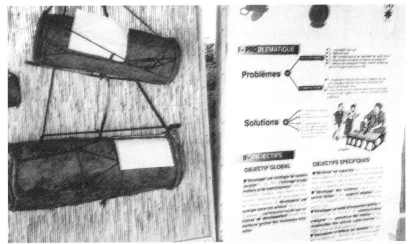

*Identifying communication objectives in relation to the problem identified and
the solutions which the community wants to experiment with, ensures that
the activities will support the community's initiative.*

of another well, to the national water program.

In a community initiative aiming to manage collectively a forest, there may be material needs such as tools to cut wood, seeds to plant new trees, access to drinkable water, etc. and again development resources are needed to address those needs. At the same time, people must understand the necessity to manage the forest if they want it to survive, and be able to take into consideration the specific needs of different categories of users. There may also be needs relating to learning different techniques, or needs relating to the setting up of a community forestry management mechanism.

To identify such needs, it is not enough to ask the question directly in a community meeting. This work needs to be done with each group of participants, both those most directly affected by the problem and those who are in a position to help resolve it. Sometimes, needs will be identified not through direct answers from community members, but through an observation of the different practices in use or by comparing the answers or lack of answers of the different groups.

Again, this identification of needs must be linked to the problem or to the goal identified previously and to the initiative to be carried out. The question which can guide us in this is the following: What do the different groups we are working with need in order to experiment with or implement a specific set of activities, which can help solve a specific problem?

Communication objectives

Communication objectives are based on the communication needs of each specific group concerned by a specific problem or a set of research activities. These objectives are identified and then prioritised. The final choice of objectives may be made on the basis of the needs that are most urgent, or those most susceptible to action. They are then defined in terms of the action which need to occur for the objectives to be achieved.

Generally, in the context of natural resource management, the objectives are linked to one or several of these communication functions: raising awareness, sharing information, facilitating learning, supporting participation, decision-making and collaborative action, mediating conflicts, influencing the policy environment.

An important aspect though is not to limit oneself to awareness-raising objectives. It may be important to raise awareness for a community management of a forest, or for a better community management of water resources. However, this objective should be accompanied by other objectives aiming to:

- develop a plan for such a management,
- set up a community mechanism to carry it forward and monitor it,

- learn specific forestry techniques (in the case of the first situation).

One question we may ask ourselves in identifying these objectives is the following: what are the results, (in terms of knowledge, attitudes, behaviour or problem-solving capacity) that each group of participants should be expected to achieve by the end of the initiative? Each of these results then constitutes an objective.

In this way, we will have a general objective, which defines the final results that we hope to accomplish, and more specific objectives relating to each of these results, which will serve as the basis for the activities to be undertaken.

It is best if these objectives can be set out in observable terms, because that will greatly facilitate subsequent evaluation. However, we should not overdo that.

For example, it may be very difficult to tell, at the end of a communication strategy for improving soil fertility, whether we have "reduced desertification risk". It will be easier to ascertain whether the specific community groups with whom the communication facilitator worked understand the process of desertification as it takes place in their own setting, whether they are aware of appropriate protective measures, and have put one or more of these into practice.

But on the other hand, to be too specific may be as problematic as to be too general. It may be more appropriate to formulate an objective as "to facilitate the understanding of causes related to a water conflict problem in the community" than to formulate it as "75% of the community members will be able to identify five causes related to the water conflict problem in the community". The latter would be a better formulation in the context of a class (pedagogical objectives) but is rather unproductive at the scale of a community.

Again, this planning exercise should be done with the participation of the various groups of participants and resource persons working with the initiative.

From communication objectives to communication activities

The next stage is to regroup the different objectives involving the same community groups and to consider the best way of supporting each group in achieving them. For each group of participants and for each objective, we should then ask ourselves what the most appropriate modes of communication are?

For example, if we want to work closely with women on water use, in many settings, it may be better to arrange first for a global meeting with husbands and wives to explain the intention, discuss the problem and then arrange for working exclusively with groups of women, than trying to isolate women for participation in communication activities.

It is on the basis of such strategic considerations that communication activities are then identified and ranked by order of priority.

It is particularly important at this point to be realistic about the feasibility issues and not to compile an endless list of activities that is too ambitious.

Step 5: Identifying appropriate communication tools

Communication tools and the planning process

Until now we have gone through a planning process which starts with identifying specific groups, their communication needs and objectives, and goes on to identify communication activities and then communication tools.

Telling stories with photographs: here farmers use communication tools to express and share their experiences. The photographs show the process they have experimented for improving their soil, using a combination of local and modern knowledge.

The process is different from when people say, "we're going to do a video, or a radio program, or a play", without knowing exactly what contribution it will make to the initiative.

Here, we want to respond to specific communication needs. We identify the communication objectives we want to attain and communication activities are developed for that purpose. Now the communication tools we are going to use in those activities are exactly that: tools. They are not the "product" or the "output". We use them to help to achieve the communication objectives we are pursuing with each category of stakeholders we are working with in the community.

The expression "Communication Tools"

Everyone is familiar with the notion of communication "media". Generally, we distinguish between the mass media (newspapers, radio, television), the traditional media (storytelling, theatres, songs), "group" media (video, photographs, posters), and community media such as short-range rural radio broadcasting.

The media, and the different forms of interpersonal communication, are our communication tools.

If we use the expression "communication tools" here, it is to stress the instrumental nature of these media: their purpose in this case is not to disseminate information, but rather to support the process of participatory communication.

In that perspective it is important to choose those communication tools which will support two-way communication and which are in relation with what we want to do and the people we want to work with.

What should we consider in selecting communication tools?

In selecting the appropriate communication tools, we need to consider three essential criteria:

Criterion 1: Community Use
Whenever possible, rely on the communication tools already in use in the local community for exchanging information and points of view or the ones they are most comfortable with.

Remember that we are not working anymore with a view to disseminate information and knowledge from a resource person (researcher or expert) to community members, but to facilitate the realization of the set of actions they decided to implement or experiment with, at the beginning of the planning process.

For example, the goal will not consist in producing a video to explain a given technology to a community but to use it as a tool for community members to discuss their own experiences with it and share their learning.

Also, whenever there is a learning situation, the use of communication tools should go hand in hand with what we have learned from adult education: we should always start from the experiences of people and we should try to build an active learning experience.

CRITERION 2: COST

Consider the cost of using the tools, the time needed to prepare the materials and the technical environment in which they are to be used (availability of electricity, appropriate premises, accessibility to participants, etc.).

A research team may think that community members would benefit from the use of local radio, but if this radio does not exist, it may not be the right option, considering those criteria. Or the costs involved in producing radio programs may be too high for the available resources.

CRITERION 3: KIND OF UTILIZATION

Select communication tools in the light of the different kinds of utilization.

Some user notes presenting some communication tools and their selection based on these criteria are presented in part 3 of this guide.

Step 6: Preparing and pre-testing communication content and materials

Involving participants in identifying and preparing communication content and materials

Participatory communication is not always associated with producing material and content. When it is however, there are some considerations to keep in mind. The use of communication tools implies not only the development of messages, content and

Involving people in identifying and producing communication content and materials: in this photograph, researchers are asking community members what communication tools they would need or like to use to share their learning with other farmers.

materials, but also a pre-testing phase aimed at confirming the effectiveness and relevance of the messages and materials, and the ways in which the tools and materials have been deployed.

You are encouraged to involve participants in identifying the communication materials. Whenever possible, it is also useful to involve them in preparing the materials. In many cases, of course, there will be a need for resource persons with the particular skills required, but it is better if this process can be monitored by some of the participants.

Pre-testing content and materials

Before finalizing any communication content or material that is to be produced, or selecting existing materials, it is important to pre-test them.

Pre-testing is a way of improving ideas and prototypes for materials by submitting them to participating group representatives and obtaining their feedback before the final production stage (or checking whether materials already produced are appropriate to the group).

This will allow us to gauge their reaction, to revise the concepts and communication materials, or perhaps to amend our strategy, if it seems unlikely to produce the desired results.

We need to be able to tell whether the concepts put forward in the communication materials are well understood by participants. We also need to know if the material is suitable and if it evokes the expected types of reactions. After pre-testing, we may want to produce more realistic illustrations, simpler texts or more explicit images.

To ensure that the communication concepts and materials are well adapted to the different groups of participants, we may ask five or six representatives from each group to give their opinion on aspects such as the following:

Content
- Understanding the content
- Accuracy of information presented
- Credibility of the people expressing themselves through the material
- The kind of reactions induced by the content

Form
- Interest evoked
- Technical quality

Materials
- Reaction to formats used
- The technical environment necessary to use the material
- The useful life of the material

FEEDBACK
- Usefulness of the material for evoking reactions and expression of viewpoints from participants.

To check the accuracy of the information presented, we may also consult one or two experts.

For pre-testing purposes, we can make drafts or outlines or samples of the materials we intend to develop. In the case of films or videos, we can simply present the concepts in the form of text, drawings and photographs.

STEP 7: Facilitating partnerships

The development of local partnerships is the key factor in the success of participatory communication activities. It is a difficult thing to do for researchers who are used to working only within their team. Even NGO workers sometimes find this a challenge. Building partnerships often require a change in attitude. This is why the researcher or practitioner should invest energies in building partnerships and involving partners and collaborators in the revision of the communication plan while she is developing a communication strategy to support the development initiative or experimentation to be carried on by the community.

Facilitating collaboration and partnerships

We can identify five types of partnerships to be developed around participatory development communication activities:

- with the community groups themselves,
- with local authorities,
- with local technical services and specialized agencies (like NGOs working in the area),

Involving local media: the local radio station had formed its own theatre group. Plays were performed, recorded and broadcasted to other communities. Feedback was then collected in the field and fed back into the process.

- with local media (rural radio or press, theatre, traditional media), and
- with the community as a whole (resource persons, local talent).

Partnership with community groups means involving them in a series of stages, from identifying problems and needs, through setting objectives and preparing a communication strategy, to implementing the activities. This requires both that the communication facilitator has an open attitude and that the participant groups be willing to learn to work in a new kind of relationship. Partnership is not something that happens automatically. In fact, the cultural context of communication has been moulded by the mass media: it is a one-way process whereby messages are beamed from a transmitter in the direction of receivers. It may take some time to become familiar with and learn to use a different approach, based on facilitating a two-way interchange.

Another type of partnership to establish is with the **local authorities**. In many settings, this partnership is necessary if one wants to work freely in the community. It can also help foster a better understanding of the development initiative and win the support needed for its successful implementation. Sometimes this can take the form of strong moral support or even of material or financial contributions to the communication activities or development initiative.

Research teams and development practitioners also need to establish an initial partnership with government **technical services** in the area, or with specialized community agencies or NGOs dealing with the issues under discussion. Such partnership is essential for the initial phase of identifying a specific development problem and its causes, and should be pursued throughout the planning and implementation of communication activities. It is particularly important that the practitioner does not attempt to substitute for these human resources in the local community, and that she establishes the conditions for true collaboration. Even when the practitioner or the member of a research team is a specialist in the discipline, she should develop partnership with the technical resources, which are tackling those issues in the community.

There is also a partnership to develop with the local mass media (rural press, rural radio) and with the traditional media (story-tellers, musicians, puppeteers, theatre troupes). This partnership is at the interface of interpersonal communication and media communication. Most initiatives are greatly enhanced by the participation and support of the media, but most researchers and development practitioners do not know how to approach them or work with them. So there really is a need at that level. Furthermore, radio, for example, can greatly assist in scaling up the work done in a given community and advocate its replication on a larger scale.

So establishing partnership with the media is crucial. But rather than turning to them for specific services on an ad hoc basis, it is far better to involve them in planning and implementing the entire activity. Here again, new relationships have to be developed and learned.

Finally, another type of partnership involves local artistic or sporting talent as well as local resource persons who can facilitate or support the communication activities outside any organizational framework. They may have particular talents or skills (photographers, graphic artists, singers, video technicians) or they may be able to contribute experience or knowledge specific to the theme of the communication.

Involving partners and collaborators in planning the communication initiative

Partnership with local technical services and specialized agencies does not happen by itself, and presupposes the learning of a culture of collaboration. This is not just simple cooperation, but a two-way process: competent resource persons will contribute to the communication activity in support of a development initiative in their field of expertise, and the technical services will in turn be able to revise their approach to various local groups. Here again, a new set of relationships must be learned. In general, we seldom find an established culture of professional collaboration among different agencies. Collaboration is often seen as an opportunity to sell services. In this respect, researchers and development practitioners should be careful to distance themselves from the notion of "project", both in their vocabulary and in their attitude. It is best to avoid this word altogether, since it is highly charged with notions of material and financial rewards.

Partners must also become familiar with the role played by the team undertaking the communication activities, and they must understand why they have been approached. They must also recognize the advantages they can draw from partnership, as well as the limitations of communication activities. The conditions governing partnership should also be negotiated, and the roles of the partners should be clearly established before proceeding. Finally, contact should be established with partners during the planning stage, so their views can be incorporated and taken into account in preparing and carrying out the strategies. The different aspects of the communication strategy (objectives, approach, required technical and financial resources) should also be discussed with each resource person. Contributions may also be sought at this point (for example, gasoline for vehicles, refreshments for participants at events, cassettes for making recordings).

The point here is not to ask resource persons to contribute their services on an ad hoc basis, but rather to involve them as collaborators in the initiative itself. It is important to enlist collaborators from the outset in identifying and discussing the communication strategy. This is particularly true when it comes to representatives of government services and the media, and resource persons that the communication facilitator hopes to involve.

Making partnership a two-way street

Local partnerships, and more specifically those with government services or community organizations, should be a two-way street. Participation in the communication process can also help officials of these services and organizations revise their own community action strategies: they can learn the methodology (particularly how to work with targeted groups) and put it into practice themselves. Participatory development communication will also help them develop a better understanding of their various target groups and evaluate their strategy.

Partnership and collaboration must therefore work in both directions: by means of such initiatives, the research team or the practitioner seeks support for developing the communication strategy and supporting the experimentation or the implementation of a community initiative. In return they offer local partners a way to examine and improve their own activities.

Intermediating

Sometimes building partnerships in the local community with other stakeholders involved in development issues can support the initiative to be carried out to resolve a specific development problem. But sometimes it is necessary to address other issues that are raised in the participatory process with the community but which are not part of the mandate of the research team or the development practitioner. Teams working on soil fertility issues may have to face for example, the problems faced by farmers with regard to accessing credit. Others may have to meet the need for literacy. Others, working in water issues for example, will confront health and hygiene needs. And finally, nearly everyone, independent of the mandate negotiated with the community at the beginning of the process, will be confronted with demands regarding material resources because of the context of poverty in which we work.

So intermediation with other structures or institutions becomes part of the work to be done and should be recognized as such. Without deviating from their mandate, the teams working on soil fertility issues and facing credit problems for example, can

Developing a communication plan together: researchers working with community members and development practitioners jointly plan and discuss the communication activities they will prepare and implement to support community initiatives.

arrange for the collaboration of other resources, or directly link farmers with representatives of credit institutions to discuss the issue and try to find some accommodation when possible. Or the development practitioner facing a demand regarding material resources can link the community with NGOs or technical services competent in dealing with the needs expressed in the process.

Step 8: Producing an implementation plan

Producing an implementation plan includes planning to undertake specific activities, identifying responsibilities and tasks, establishing the time line for the communication strategy and preparing the budget for each activity.

It can be useful at this point to review the preliminary steps of communication planning:

Problem or goal and development initiative

First the researcher or the development practitioner and the community have identified a specific problem they want to tackle. An initiative to experiment with a set of solutions or actions was then decided.

Specific groups

The different community groups, policy makers and other development stakeholders affected by the problem or involved in the solution have been identified. The researcher or practitioner, together with community representatives will then identify the specific groups with whom they will work with in priority.

Communication needs and objectives

The needs of each of these groups in terms of communication, information, awareness, learning new knowledge or new techniques, etc., have been identified and prioritized. Based on the needs selected from this list, communication objectives have been identified in a way that spells out what is to be accomplished with each specific group at the end of the communication initiative.

First draft of an implementation plan

To plan the sequencing and the follow-up of the communication activities and to identify areas of responsibility, it may be useful to organize the different choices that have been made in a table such as the one shown below, where each planned communication activity is linked to an objective:

Communica-tion Objectives	Activities	Communica-tion Tools	Material Require-ments	Resource Persons	Budget Require-ments	Implemen-tation Period
1	1.1					
	1.2					
	1.3					
	1.4					
2						

Planning the follow-up of the activities

We are now ready to plan the follow-up of the activities. Some call it a monitoring plan and use it as a reference tool during monitoring and evaluation. This planning will allow us to determine whether activities are being conducted as and when planned. To do this we recast and complete the table by identifying the following in greater detail:

- The order and sequence of activities.
- The timing and the duration, details of date, time and place.
- The individuals responsible for each activity.
- The partners and resource persons involved, other persons invited.
- The material requirements (e.g. room, chairs, documents, film projector).
- Budget needs (e.g., cost of gasoline for getting to the activity site).

This table can be used for forecasting the activities before they are carried out, as well as for monitoring the overall performance of the activities.

Communication objectives	Activities	Communication on tools	Material Requirements	Resource Persons	Budget Requirements	Implementation Period
1	1.1					
	1.2					
	1.3					
	1.4					
2						

Implementation Period	Location	Person Responsible	Observations
1	1.1		
	1.2		
	1.3		
	1.4		
2			

Establishing the time line

The preparation of this follow-up plan leads us to identify the period of time over which the activities will be conducted.

It is important to establish a realistic time schedule for the various activities: making initial local contacts, deepening our knowledge of the problem, planning communication activities, carrying them out, and evaluating them.

This schedule should also be consistent with three different calendars:

- The periods of availability of the different community groups the research team or practitioner intends to work with.
- The agenda of the technical agents involved in the activities.
- The moments of availability of the research team or practitioners themselves.

Thus, there are several elements that must be taken into consideration:

- The timing of activities.
- The availability of participants and resource persons.
- The research team or practitioner's own availability.
- The availability of required materials and equipment.

We must never forget that in situations where travel and communication are difficult, and where material resources are scarce, the most modest activity often takes much longer than initially expected. When we also have to coordinate a set of activities involving a number of partners, things become really complicated. It is best, therefore, to be modest in your ambitions.

The support budget

When the time comes to prepare the support budget for the communication strategy and each of its activity, we must think carefully about the notion of cost. The idea is not to build up an impressive budget, but to encourage groups of participants to take responsibility for activities. This is why we speak of a support budget rather than an operational budget.

This point goes hand in hand with earlier comments about changing mentalities and ways of doing things in connection with the implementation of local development "projects". It is important that community groups involved in the process participate in putting together the means of experimenting or implementing a given solution: it is the only way in which communities can reclaim the initiative they develop as their own.

Preparing the budget

Preparing a budget involves several different stages.

We must first identify the human and material resources needed to carry out each activity: resource persons and physical resources; materials and equipment, fuel needs (exchange visits, travel by resource persons), consumable supplies (photographic film, paper, batteries, ink, poster paint, etc.).

The participation of resource persons should not usually imply costs chargeable to the budget, except for travel to the locale of the activity. This being said, in some countries, resource persons working in many technical services are paid so little, that it makes sense offering compensation for their participation, even if it is in theory part of their mandate. This must be examined case by case and not constitute an automatic process.

For material resources, we need to ask which materials we can borrow, which we need to buy, and those that we can produce. Then we must identify which activities entail specific costs.

Secondly, we must review each of these needs, weigh their importance, and ask ourselves if there is an alternative. We should think carefully about what expenses are really necessary. For example, renting chairs for a meeting or providing snacks or meals for participants can hardly be said to be essential. Nor can that be said of the costs of developing several films to document the activity, when one film would do.

Third, for each of these needs, we must identify those that can be covered by the researcher's or practitioner's own organization, by the budget of the research team, or by contributions from various partners and collaborators. Some costs may be borne by the municipality or local agencies, or by the participants in the communication activities. Participants can often prepare a snack, for example. The mayor or the prefect may be able to provide physical premises. It is important to involve local players in supporting the cost of these activities. Even if the contribution is minimal or symbolic, it allows participants and resource persons to feel a sense of ownership over the activity, and not to regard themselves merely as beneficiaries or as invited guests.

Finally, we must estimate and add in the expenses involved in covering the material resources needed for each activity, and ask whether they are worth the cost. We may often find that we must review our choices, in the light of the resources that we have been able to assemble.

Step 9: Monitoring and evaluating the communication strategy and documenting the development or research process

Why evaluate?

During the intervention phase of the research or development initiative, the communication component will focus on the implementation, monitoring, and evaluation of the communication strategy and on documenting the participatory development or research process.

The production of a monitoring plan and of an evaluation framework linked to it, will help everyone involved in the activities to monitor what is being accomplished and facilitate its evaluation. The joint elaboration of such a plan by all stakeholders using simple methods such as brainstorming, observation and visualisation can be very helpful. However, the most crucial consideration here is the way in which researchers and practitioners approach the evaluation process together with their partners – the community members and the other development stakeholders – so that the evaluation process becomes a learning experience for everyone involved in it.

We define evaluation as a judgment based on the information collected. There are two main reasons for conducting an evaluation:

- To find out if we are on the right track or whether we need to adjust our course during the execution of the activity.
- To find out if we have achieved our original objectives, and if the results have had an impact on the problem identified at the outset.

During the implementation period evaluation allows us to:

- Determine whether we are on track toward achieving the initial objectives.
- Identify the major difficulties encountered and the corrective actions required.

This evaluation is generally done at the same time as monitoring, which assesses the progress and realization of activities and the participation in the activities. Many researchers and practitioners address the two sets of considerations within the same process, since they can be done at the same time.

Rating the level of participation, understanding and feeling: simple evaluation techniques are useful for learning from the activities and improving their potential to support community initiatives.

At the end of the process evaluation allows us to:

- Determine whether we have achieved our objectives and to what extent.
- Assess the degree to which our activities have had the desired impact on the problem or the development initiative that we wanted to address.
- Draw lessons from the experience, identify ways of improving performance, and make recommendations for future activities.

In the context of participatory development communication activities, it is useful to integrate these two aspects into a continuous process of monitoring and evaluation.

The aspect related to impact is of course difficult to measure. It depends first on how we define development, in terms of processes or observable change. It also depends on the scale of time we use. Most of the changes nurtured by PDC, in terms of attitude and behaviour change, participation, or knowledge acquisition and utilization, take a long time to evolve. It may be useful at that stage to agree on measuring specific indicators that may point to those changes.

What is the purpose of evaluation and who will use the results?

Information produced from an evaluation can be useful to stakeholders of various kinds:

- Those responsible for developing the communication strategy. This information is essential to the researchers or practitioners responsible for the communication activities, to the partners involved, and to the community groups involved, to help them along the way in completing their project, and to recognize, at the end of the activities, the results that have been achieved as well as the lessons that can be learned for the future.
- Members of the community, in particular the authorities and technical services responsible for the areas addressed by the communication activities, to help them carry out their responsibilities more effectively.
- Donors, whether these are local organizations or outside development agencies. Those who contribute to such activities need to know if their investment was worthwhile and if it has served its objective.

- Public audience or the development community. Some of the information produced during evaluation can also be of interest to other local community groups, other potential development partners, and other potential donors. At the national level, it can serve to publicize results among other community groups, and to the population at large.

Who should be involved?

When we speak of evaluation, we generally think of an expert brought in from outside, who prepares a report based on a tour of the field. Donors who want to know if their money has been well used generally commission such evaluations.

Yet in the context of participatory development communication, it can be very useful to undertake an evaluation that involves the various players who have taken part in the activities. Participatory communication activities are intended to facilitate participation by local groups in initiatives designed to help them develop and improve living conditions. It is therefore natural that those involved in the initiative should be the first to try to understand the approach and recognize its results.

Thus, it is the researcher or the practitioner who goes through the evaluation process, together with members of the community groups involved and the local partners involved in the activities.

This does not prevent us from drawing upon technical resources to help us prepare the evaluation plan or produce the information-gathering tools. Such resources are often very useful in helping to plan an evaluation, to encourage the sharing of viewpoints, and to summarize and analyze the data. But the responsibility remains that of all the players involved.

Nor does this approach prevent you from resorting to other kinds of external evaluation for specific aspects, nor from carrying out more precise measurements of some points or validating the results of a participatory evaluation.

What should be evaluated?

We should remember that evaluation as considered here is a continuous, ongoing process throughout each stage of an activity. We must try therefore to incorporate both these aspects that we want to evaluate at the end of the activity, and those that we want to assess during the course of its implementation.

We can never evaluate everything that has been done from the beginning to the end. At all times we must be selective about what is essential. To do this, we must identify, from among all the possible evaluation questions, those where answers are required. We may consider three levels of evaluation:

- The process: everything that was done from the outset: planning and implementation of activities.
- The results of communication activities.
- The observable impact of activities on the problem or on the development initiative: do the results contribute to resolving the problem that was posed at the outset, or to supporting the development initiative that was identified?

For each of these levels, we will now:

- Identify what we want to evaluate and formulate the questions we need to answer.
- Identify the information needed to answer those questions.
- Identify a procedure for collecting that information.

How to plan a participatory evaluation?

The first stage consists in formulating the evaluation questions by means of discussion with everyone involved in the communication strategy: research team or practitioners, local partners, resource persons and groups of participants. This involves a sorting process: identifying those points on which we want to render an opinion, and formulating them in terms of questions.

Secondly, we will try to identify the information needed to respond to each of these questions.

Thirdly, we must determine where to find that information.

This is demanding work. It is highly advisable to enlist the assistance of a resource person and to moderate the debate effectively. During the discussion, we must also be careful to ensure that everyone has a chance to speak and express her viewpoint freely. Finally, we must divide up tasks and assign responsibilities for evaluating the degree to which objectives have been achieved, or for seeking out information from the sources identified.

Examples of evaluation questions relating to participatory communication

By way of example, here are a few questions that may be useful in evaluating your communication strategy. You may wish to use them directly or adapt them to your own context. Also, many of these questions can be rephrased in order to evaluate the process of the initiative itself, and not only the communication strategy supporting it.

You can also use this example to review the planning of your communication strategy.

Q1. OVERALL, IS THE COMMUNICATION STRATEGY APPROPRIATE TO THE DEVELOPMENT PROBLEM IDENTIFIED?

Information needed:

Do the communication activities:
- Promote development efforts to address a development problem in the community?
- Reinforce such efforts undertaken by community groups or partners?
- Respond to the concerns of community groups and partners?

Potential sources of information:
- Review of the plans for the communication strategy.
- Discussion with the community groups and partners involved.

Q2. IN SUPPORTING THE DEVELOPMENT EFFORT IDENTIFIED, IS THE COMMUNICATION STRATEGY PURSUING THE RIGHT GOAL?

Information needed:
- Does the community recognize the problem as important?
- Have the causes of the problem been analyzed?
- What are the chances of success of the development initiative undertaken?

Potential sources of information:
- Discussions with the competent technical services in the community.
- Discussion with the local people.
- Consultation of documentation and statistics on the problem.
- In some cases, photographs or records illustrating the problem.

Q3. ARE THE COMMUNITY GROUPS INVOLVED THE MOST APPROPRIATE ONES IN TERMS OF THE PROBLEM POSED AND THE DEVELOPMENT ACTION IDENTIFIED?

Information needed:
- Were those specific groups identified on the basis of common characteristics?
- Are they representative of the people most affected by the problem, or those who could help find a solution?
- Do the social and geographic conditions in the local community allow access to the identified community groups by the research team or the practitioner?

Potential sources of information:
- Discussions with the competent local technical services.
- Discussions with the local people.
- Review of the plans for the communication activities.
- Consultation of documentation on the conduct of the communication activities (activity reports, weekly logbooks).

Q4. IS THE COMMUNITY PARTICIPATING ACTIVELY IN THE COMMUNICATION ACTIVITIES?

Information needed:
- Are various players involved in the activities?
- Have local partnerships been established with:
    - a. technical services,
    - b. the authorities,
    - c. the media,
    - d. other resource persons?

- Are partners investing their own human, physical or financial resources in the initiative?
- Are the identified community groups active in the communication activities?
- Was the development initiative decided in coordination with all the players involved or in response to a local request?
- Has care been taken to ensure that researchers or practitioners do not substitute themselves for the competent local technical services?

Potential sources of information:
- Examination of cooperation agreements and procedures with partners.
- Discussion with all the players involved.

Q5. Are the communication objectives being pursued the right ones?

Information needed:
- Were the objectives identified on the basis of the identified groups' needs?
- Were the objectives formulated in terms of expected results?
- Are the objectives realistic in the light of local conditions?
- Will achievement of the objectives pursued by the communication strategy contribute to the success of the development initiative it is intended to support?

Potential sources of information:
- Review of planning documentation.
- Discussion with partners and specific community groups.

Q6. Is the communication strategy well articulated?

Information needed:
- Does each activity correspond to an objective?
- Do activities grouped under the same objective contribute to its realization?
- Were the characteristics of the different community groups involved taken into account in preparing the activities?
- Are activities proceeding as planned?
- Are members of community groups, partners, resource persons participating in the activities?
- Was the schedule of activities established with due regard to the availability of the specific community groups involved and the planning schedules of partners?

Potential sources of information:
- Review of planning documentation for the communication strategy.
- Comparison of the number of activities planned and the number of activities conducted; planned and actual timing and duration.
- Record of the number of participants in each activity.
- Effective participation of partners in the activities.
- Observations on the progress of activities.

Q7. Are the communication activities really participatory?

Information needed:
- Did community groups and partners participate in planning the initiative?
- Are community groups expressing themselves freely and often during communication activities?

- Are field workers and resource persons helping the participants to express themselves?
- During meetings, does everyone have a chance to speak and express herself?

Potential sources of information:
- Review of planning documentation for the communication strategy.
- Discussion with participating community groups and partners.
- Observations made during the activities.

Q8. ARE THE COMMUNICATION TOOLS APPROPRIATE TO THE COMMUNITY GROUPS INVOLVED AND TO THE COMMUNICATION OBJECTIVES?

Information needed:
- What communication media, materials and community communication channels are being used?
- Has thought been given to the way they are used:
  - » To sensitize local people to a development problem?
  - » To facilitate knowledge and information acquisition by community groups?
  - » To illustrate a desirable attitude or mode of behaviour?
  - » To document the solution of a specific problem?
  - » To facilitate the expression of viewpoints by community groups?
  - » To facilitate debate over the different viewpoints of community groups and technical partners?
  - » To monitor the development initiative?
  - » To help the authorities or technical partners to understand the circumstances under which community groups are living?

> » To document the planning and conduct of the communication strategy and the development initiative?
> » For other objectives?

- Do the community groups understand the contents and messages?
- Is the communication material adapted to them?
- Are the communication tools effective?
- Are the communication channels used suitable to the community groups and to local realities?
- Are materials available as and when needed?

Potential sources of information:
- Review of planning documentation for the communication initiative.
- Pre-testing of the communication contents and materials.
- Observations on the use of communication tools and materials.

Q9. ARE THE INITIAL CHOICES REGARDING THE PREPARATION AND IMPLEMENTATION OF THE COMMUNICATION ACTIVITIES STILL RELEVANT?

Information needed:
- Are all players performing their tasks satisfactorily?
- Are the material resources sufficient and adapted for proper conduct of the activities? Are the initial choices that were made with respect to community groups, objectives and activities still relevant to the needs initially identified?

Potential sources of information:
- Monitoring of activities.
- Fund management.

- Review of planning documentation and discussion with partners and community groups.

Q10. Have the communication objectives been achieved, and to what extent?

Information needed:
This information will vary depending on the objectives in question. In each case, we must first define what we need to know in order to determine whether the objectives have been achieved and to what extent.

Objectives relating to the acquisition of information, knowledge or to the development of attitudes:
- The capacity of community groups to provide adequate responses to the questions posed or to a given situation.
- A comparison of responses (information or attitudes) given before and after the activity.

Objectives relating to the development of competencies:
- The capacity of community groups to demonstrate a specific skill.
- The capacity to apply acquired knowledge and skills to resolving a problem.

Objectives relating to participation in a development initiative:
- The effective participation in an initiative by community groups.
- Documentation of the different forms of that participation.

Potential sources of information:
- Knowledge acquisition: This information can generally be found in discussions, small tests or informal interviews.

- Attitudes and Competencies: Observations, problem resolution or participation in a concrete action.
- Participation in a development initiative: Relevant documentation; statistics, in some cases, photographs or video records of the impact of the development initiative on the community.

Q11. ARE THE COMMUNICATION OBJECTIVES AND STRATEGY LIKELY TO HAVE AN IMPACT IN THE COMMUNITY?

Information needed:
- Will the communication activities help to find solutions to the concerns of community groups?
- Will they help the participants to contribute to resolving the problem identified at the outset?
- Have there been any unexpected consequences or results?

Potential information sources:
- Observations.
- Evidence provided by community groups and partners.
- Success of the development initiative.

Q12. SHOULD WE:
- Proceed with the communication strategy as planned?
- Make changes?
- Terminate it?

Documenting activities

Documenting the development intervention or research activities, as well as the communication activities, is a complementary task to monitoring and evaluation.

It is as if we had to give an account of everything that we have accomplished. That account must also include all the difficulties and problems encountered, and the solutions found. This is what we call documenting activities. One way of doing it is to use a weekly "logbook", or a record of activities, in which we document all the events that occurred during the week, the observations from the monitoring activities and any personal comments.

Another important issue is ensuring the documentation of communication and development or research activities. Both categories compose the participatory process set in motion. This aspect is often forgotten during the excitement of implementing the activities and the story that is written after completion, often misses out on key aspects of what took place.

Ideally, the account of the research or development initiative and the communication activities that supported them should include the difficulties encountered, solutions experimented and

Planning to share and apply results: sharing results refers to making information available in different formats to different groups of users and collecting feedback; applying the results helps in extending the process to other communities and in advocating for participatory approaches. Participation of the different community groups in this decision-making process is critical.

the evolution of the partnership between researchers, practitioners, community members and other stakeholders.

One way of doing this is to use a weekly logbook, or a record of activities, in which we record all events that occurred during the week, the observations from the monitoring activities and any personal comments. We may also discover other means of documenting: a photograph album, for example, highlighting communication activities with captions and commentaries for each photograph, or a collection of video sequences on the various activities which took place.

Step 10: Planning the sharing and utilization of results

At the end of the participatory research or development cycle, community members, researchers and practitioners assess together the results of their work. Sometimes, this assessment will point to a redefinition of the problem or solution identified at the beginning of the cycle. Or it may lead them to reconsider some of the choices made during the planning phase. When the intervention has led to the desired results the next step involves the sharing of this knowledge with different groups of stakeholders as well as scaling efforts with other communities or other groups of stakeholders.

Knowledge sharing refers to making information available in different formats to different groups of users and asking for their feedback. It is one step ahead of a simple dissemination of information. Scaling efforts usually focus on one of the following activities of extension, outreach or advocacy: extending the process to other groups in the community or to another community; replicating the process at a larger scale, involving a larger number of communities; using the knowledge produced at the community level to act on a policy level (influencing policy-makers or networking with organizations).

These two sets of activities introduce a new planning exercise. The idea is not only to transmit specific information to other stakeholders but also to identify the conditions in which they could use such information and knowledge to foster change.

The first step will consist in determining the goal(s) to pursue. Researchers, practitioners and community members will then use the same logic as the one used for planning the communication strategy:

The problem resolution or the goal to which the research or development activity is contributing:
- What is the relevant knowledge that should be produced by the research or development activity?

The specific groups concerned:
- Apart from the participants, who could make use of the research results or of the knowledge about what has been achieved in the community?
- What are the appropriate communication strategies for reaching them?
- What are the appropriate channels and tools of communication for each of them?

The communication needs:
- What are their needs in terms of information and communication?
- What will they need in order to be able to use the information?

The objectives:
- What should be the objectives of the dissemination or the scaling up activity, for each of the specific groups that we want to reach?

Asking those questions at the onset of activities also means that we can involve representatives of the different groups identified in the research or development activity. This usually helps in increasing the receptivity of those groups after the process is completed.

The sharing of the relevant information and the accompanying extension inside a given community or in neighboring local communities will be facilitated if during the research, participating farmers are trained to explain to others what they are involved in and if appropriate communication channels are identified for doing so.

Scaling up at the level of policy makers will also be facilitated if during the research or development activity specific key persons are identified and if they are made aware of the process at work and invited to share questions or suggestions. The idea is not only to inform them of a specific content but also to identify the conditions in which they could use such information and knowledge to foster change.

In both cases, the process will be reinforced if during the research or development activity, for each specific group, appropriate modes of approach and of presenting the information are identified. This means seeking ways of presenting the information from the angle acceptable to these specific groups, with the type of format they use, and considering the appropriate timing and context. The way research teams and development organizations usually present their work is generally not intended to reach potential users and the format used for this purpose does not take into account users' preferences and needs. The angle must be shifted from information content to user's needs.

This planning step is the beginning of a new cycle that may start a new intervention or focus on disseminating the lessons learned during the research or development activity. Gathering a few ideas on this issue at the beginning of the process will help to develop it during the research or development activity. It will also help to review the different choices made during the planning of the participatory development communication initiative.

Concluding remarks

To conclude this part of the guide, here are some related considerations: 1. The management aspects associated with the use of such a model and 2. The operational aspects related to the management culture of donor organizations.

Management aspects

THE MANAGEMENT CULTURE

This model demands careful revisiting of the management culture of the organization or the research team who is getting involved in such a process. Participation must also exist at that level. If all decisions are taken by the leader or the director of the group, without any participation to this decision-making process by the team members and field agents, then this internal contradiction will no doubt limit the facilitation of horizontal communication between community members and other stakeholders. In other words, we can only preach effectively what we practice.

The change of attitudes involved in using communication to facilitate a participatory development process has its corollary at the level of the team or organization leading the process. Participation in the decision-making process and knowledge sharing are as important inside the group or organization as they are at the level of the communities.

MANAGEMENT TASKS

The use of the model also involves management tasks which must be carefully taken care of. These include sensitization among the research team members or the development organization agents and field agents on the different aspects of PDC; explanation of the PDC process to community members and other stakeholders, training of team members and community facilitators; collection of feedback, identification of the decision-making process inside the group, identification of the modalities and responsibilities related to the documentation of the process, budget considerations, etc. At each step they must be identified and planned.

The importance of team preparation
The importance of initial training and preparation of team members in the use of PDC must be underlined. The kind of interaction researchers and practitioners will have with the local people – the capacity to listen, for example, or to help people talk about what they really think will have a direct influence on the kind of participation which will be nurtured.

Operational aspects in relation to donor organizations

The implementation of participatory development communication has the same constraints as the participatory development process it supports: it demands time, resources and practical modalities that can only come from a negotiation with the donor organizations involved.

At the beginning of a project
In the traditional development culture, financial support comes after revision and acceptance of a formal proposal, whether it is a research for development proposal or a development project proposal. In order to go through the different levels of revision and acceptance, such a proposal must be clear and complete.

The development problem or goal must be clearly identified and justified, the objectives outlined with precision and all the activities detailed. The full budget of course must figure in the proposal with all its budget notes.

Although some organizations are rethinking this process over and promoting a program orientation instead of a project orientation, in most of the cases, this is the situation we face. It is important to put this issue on the agenda of donor organizations and to demand the revision of such a process: if we want to develop a participatory development process and have community members and other stakeholders have their say at all phases of the process, starting with the identification and the planning phases, this means that we need time and resources to do so.

In the meantime, we can identify two modalities that can be proposed to the donor organization. The first one consists in putting together a pre-proposal that will seek to identify and plan the project with all stakeholders. The second modality – which is really a second choice, in case the first one is not possible – consists in building the proposal in a way that will permit its revision with community members and other stakeholders.

CHANGES DURING IMPLEMENTATION

Participation brings changes. A participatory development or research process cannot be planned the same way planning is done for the construction of a road: as participation is facilitated and more feedback is gathered, more consensuses are developed and decisions are made, things change. This is why it is always an iterative process and we must have the possibility of changing plans as we go along in order to better attain the objectives that have been identified.

This must also be discussed with the donor organizations involved, since traditionally, once a proposal was accepted, nothing could change.

HOW LONG DOES IT REALLY TAKE?

The length of the activities is another problem we face. Often, proposals have to be developed on a two or three year's frame. But participation takes time and this span is often just enough to really start the process. So even if the expected results have not been realized, it is necessary to identify the progress made by the research and development activity, and build the cases for the continuation of support. This underlines also the importance of a continuous evaluation mechanism set up during the implementation of the process.

Tools

Using communication tools with a participatory approach

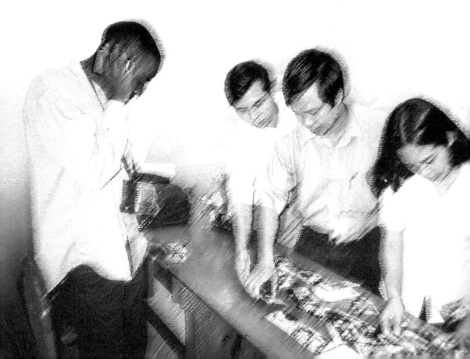

Tools

Introduction

In the previous section of this guide, we discussed the identification of communication tools in relation to three sets of criteria:

- communication tools already in use in the local community,
- costs, time and technical conditions of use, and
- various kinds of utilization.

We stressed that we are not using media with a view to disseminate information and knowledge from a resource person (researcher or expert) to community members, but to facilitate the realization of the set of actions a community decides to implement, in order to act on a given development problem.

Where there is some learning to do, we are reminded that the use of communication tools should go hand in hand with what we have learned from adult education: we should always start from the experiences of people and build an active learning experience.

In this third part of the guide, we will first present some user's notes on examples of communication tools that are often used in the context of communicating with local communities, with a participatory approach. Of course, this list is by no way exhaustive. But we will see that we will find the same elements again and again, independently of the tool itself and that they can be applied to other communication tools as well.

In a second section, we will consider usages related to different kinds of utilization (the third criterion of selection).

Types of communication tools in PDC

Generally, we distinguish between mass media (newspapers, radio, television), traditional media (storytelling, theatres, songs), "group" media (video, photographs, posters) and community media such as short-range rural radio broadcasting. The media, and the different forms of interpersonal communication, are our communication tools. The following describes some of the tools and techniques you may wish to use in your communication strategy. It may be useful to remember that often the use of more than one approach, tool or medium can strengthen your approach so these should not be viewed in isolation or as independent of one another.

Interpersonal communication tools

DISCUSSION AND DEBATE

Group discussion and debate are widely used. They are so common that we seldom think of them as communication tools. But if we do, we can greatly enhance their utilization. As communication tools, they should support a given activity (in this case, generally a community meeting), in order to reach a specific objective. Usually, the objective will consist of raising an issue publicly, stimulating awareness and preparing for other activities.

From large debates to small groups discussions: the effectiveness of large group discussions and debates resides in their complementarity with other activities, such as discussions with smaller and more focused groups.

A large group discussion is not always the best tool though to facilitate participation. Often, only certain categories of people will talk, offer their arguments or ask questions. In many settings, young people or women will not talk in front of the older men. And of course, many topics cannot be discussed openly in public.

The effectiveness of discussion and debate resides in its complementarity with other activities, for example discussions with smaller and more focused groups.

VISIONING SESSIONS

The same applies to visioning sessions of a film or video. Usually, these sessions are organized during a public meeting where resource persons talk about a given issue, and where, after the projection, a discussion is organized. This tool is very effective in raising awareness on a specific issue, or to introduce knowledge or behavior elements, but as a single activity, it has little potential to stimulate participation to work out some solutions.

Again, the effectiveness of the tool is linked with the organization of other activities, again with smaller and more focused groups.

FOCUS GROUP DISCUSSIONS

A focus group discussion is held with a small number of people (7–10) who share similar characteristics. The information obtained through this technique is considered valid for other community members who demonstrate those characteristics.

The discussion evolves along the lines of a discussion guide, prepared before hand, but the questions are open-ended. The idea is to enable every participant to express his/her opinions on a given topic.

In many cases, a focus group discussion can also evolve in a strategy-developing activity, with each participant contributing not only to the identification of a problem, causes or solutions, but also in a strategy which could facilitate community participation to the resolution of that problem and the experimentation of the potential solutions.

PRA TECHNIQUES

Participatory rural appraisal techniques are well documented and used in the field. The exercises can include the use of different techniques like collective mapping of the local area, developing a time line, ranking the importance of problems inside a matrix, wealth ranking, doing observation walks, using Venn diagrams, producing seasonability diagrams, etc.

As communication tools, they give us a lot of of information in a limited time span about the characterization of natural resources in a given area and basic social, economic and political information, in order to plan a development or research project. As such, they are powerful tools for facilitating the participation of community members. But as mentioned earlier, they can also be used restrictively, when the different techniques are not fully in the hands of the participants and remain techniques used by the research team only to gather information for their own purposes.

The main idea in using PRA is to collect information quickly with the participation of community members and to share it so that everyone becomes empowered by that information and can participate better in the analysis and decision-making processes. When this does not happen, and when researchers or development practitioners go back with the information without nurturing this empowerment process, the technique is not applied as it should. In fact, such a process can be detrimental because researchers and practitioners then think that they are doing participatory work, when, in fact community members are only "being participated".

ROLE-PLAYING

Role-playing can be a very interesting way to facilitate participation in a small group, identify attitudes and collect views and perceptions. In a role-play, two to five people take a specific identity and play the interaction between the characters. It is interesting when the situation asks for one character to make a case before the other ones or try to influence them.

As an example, one character could take the role of a researcher coming to the community, and another would play a community member. Each would simulate a situation in which the researcher engages in a dialogue with the community member to identify her communication needs regarding a specific natural resource management initiative.

After the play, a discussion follows. Each participant explains what happens in her group and how she felt in the guise of her character interacting with the other character. The facilitator underlines the main ideas related to the topic of discussion and links the exercise with the topic of discussion. Afterward, the participants and the facilitator evaluate if they reached the objective of the activity.

VISITS, TOURS, WORKSHOPS AND EXHIBITIONS

Home visits are an excellent way to raise awareness on a given topic and to collect the views of people on a given problem. Often, people who will not speak openly in a community meeting, or who will not participate in it, will be more at ease to share views and information in the context of their home or their field.

In the context of rural poor, it is often more effective when contact farmers instead of the research team itself make the visits, or when contact farmers accompany the research team.

Tours and visits by farmers to other farmers are useful to demonstrate some solutions, which have been used in other settings, and also to raise the motivation to try them out and experiment with them. But to be more effective, they should be prepared by the farmers who are going to visit, after many discussions on the problems they face and the solutions they could implement, instead of having farmers participate in a tour by itself.

The organization of a workshop on a given topic is useful to present and discuss specific technologies, which can support solutions to a given problem, or to assemble similarly minded people in order to develop a common strategy. It is however often more effective regrouping resource persons and collaborators from the community than community members themselves. Farmers often will not feel at ease in the context of a workshop given in the city, and the poorest and more marginalized people certainly will not come. So attention must be paid to the issue of who is at ease with the formula and who is not.

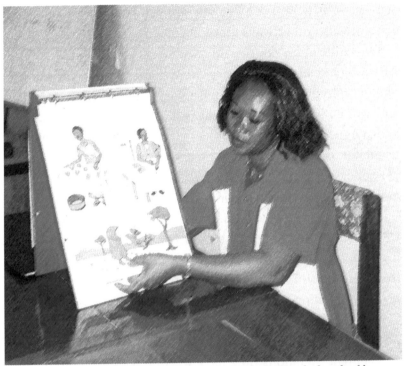

Using pictures to illustrate stories: pictures or photographs can also be utilized by participating groups to identity problematic situations, tell stories, support discussion on problems and solutions.

Finally, on-farm exhibitions and on-farm experimental plots, are more effective than exhibitions or plots at an experimental station. They are however are more difficult to organize, except if contact farmers and participating resource organizations identify them as a workable strategy and help in their realization.

"Group" media tools

Photography, drawings, flip charts

When considering using photography (or drawings), we usually think of taking pictures to illustrate what we want to discuss with other people, and use them during a visioning session, or as cards or posters. It is in fact a very flexible and supportive tool. But there are also other ways to use this tool.

One utilization consists of producing what people in West Africa have called *boîte à image* (flip chart). It is a succession of photographs or drawings that tell a story with three to ten pictures, and without any text. The images illustrate problem situations, and situations where the problem is resolved. It is used with the facilitator asking people what they see in the images. This tool is very effective in stimulating discussion, comparing points of view and developing consensus on a given issue.

The images can be drawn, printed or glued on paper or cloth.

The same process can be used by making a game of cards from those photographs or drawings and distributing the cards from one person to another, each trying to identify the image and commenting on the situation.

Another interesting utilization consists in giving disposable photo cameras to people in the field, asking them to photograph problematic situations they have to cope with or solutions they would like to see adopted and multiplied. An exhibition is made and discussions are conducted to identify strategies for action.

Similarly, photographs can be used with a discussion where people put forth their points of view with the help of what they illustrated, or to present a "before" and an "after" situation.

They are also powerful tools in the context of home visits, where they can be used to ask people what they see in the pictures and how they feel about the situation.

Posters and banners

Posters and banners are often used to raise awareness on a topic. As such they are not very effective in facilitating participation. It is important to combine them with interactive activities with community members. At that point they can be used as the flip chart process, instead of being just glued on a specific spot.

This being said, sometimes the realization of posters or of banners by community members can become a rich communication activity. For example, it can be quite effective with children, in order to raise awareness on a specific issue, or with farmers, in order to illustrate a given technology. In the latter, a resource person will work with the research team and community members to develop the poster along the guidelines of community members. The discussion along this activity is often very rich and productive.

VIDEO RECORDINGS

Today, digital video cameras make the use of video simple. They come with batteries that can last up to 7 or 8 hours, and can fit in a small backpack. They also have a screen that can be used not only to capture but also to show immediately the images to a small group of people. They are very easy to learn to operate and handle and make a good tool that community members can use by themselves.

As in the case of photography, video is usually used to illustrate a given problem or to demonstrate a given solution, by way of a program put together by the research team or produced elsewhere.

In cases where the document is produced by the research team, it is always more effective when it is done in a participatory way, including community members, in the planning, scenario development and realization.

Video is also more effective when it positions a problem and documents the causes without suggesting solutions. Those are to come from participants viewing the documentary.

As in the example of disposable cameras, it can also be a tool put in the hands of community members for them to show an aspect of a problem or solution, or record a "video letter".

A powerful utilization of video is what is known as the "Fogo Process" (the name comes from a Canadian island where it was first used). In this process, video is used to introduce an issue and is followed by a community discussion. The discussion is captured and shown to the community afterward where it triggers other discussions to bring forth a consensus for action.

In some contexts, the discussion of the issue by a community can also be shown to other communities, where the discussion is also recorded, etc.

Audio recordings

Audio recording can be used to capture the views of community members and stir a discussion afterward on these views. The recording can be played on tape recorders in the context of a community meeting or small group discussions, but it can also be broadcast on the radio when such collaboration has been achieved.

Audio recordings of songs and dances and the use of small audio players can also be effective tools for community members working with the research team to reach other members of their communities.

Audiocassette forums have also been used with some success. In this approach, tape recorders and cassettes are given to specific community groups, who decide on their content and discuss the problems and potential solutions to implement.

"Traditional" media tools

Theatre

The same considerations can be said of using theatre or other traditional media: it must be complementary to a process involving a set of interactive activities. Usually, theatre is used to raise awareness on a given issue. A play will often attract a large

Women playing men's roles: in this photograph, women farmers are presenting a theatre-debate on the issue of soil fertility. In such a setting, they can act out men's roles and attitudes and bring forward social issues related to a problem and its solutions, which they are unable to do in a formal community meeting.

number of people in the rural areas, but will not do much by itself to accompany a community initiative to resolve a given problem. It must be part of a global strategy and like other communication tools, contribute to the identification of a given development problem and a concrete initiative set up by the community.

Theatre debate (where a debate with the audience follows the play) and theatre forum (where some parts of the play are played again by audience members, usually to try to convince a character of the play to change her behavior) are powerful techniques used to address critical issues. But again, they must be linked to a longer-term initiative in order to accompany a development initiative in the community.

Another strategy is to have specific community groups participate in the writing and production of the play. When the play addresses specific problems and demonstrates useful solutions, the message is much more convincing when the actors are people from the community.

Songs, music, sayings, stories

Songs and music are powerful tools, whether they are used to create an ambience or produced in a way to deliver a message, they can greatly facilitate a process of sharing points of view and contribute to awareness raising. Again, they are only tools.

Sayings and proverbs have also been used in order to facilitate discussion on a given topic. Stories, especially hiatus stories, which have to be filled in the middle or completed at

Traditional media as powerful communication to researchers and practitioners should identify th traditional media existing in a given community and give them preference in their choice of communication tools, not only to address the community, but to enable community groups to express their views and opinions.

the end also can create an ambience, raise awareness and facilitate group discussions.

"Mass" media tools

Rural radio

As everyone recognizes, rural radio is an especially appropriate tool for reaching large groups, or groups beyond the immediate vicinity. Many producers working with rural radio are aware of participatory communication and will steer clear of the conventional "journalistic" approach. For example, they will attempt to include discussion panels in their broadcasting, and will do their best to make local voices heard.

There are two important provisos, however, for using radio successfully: first, it is important to enlist a producer (or the broadcast authorities) in the initiative and work with her in planning the entire communication process. This means an ongoing cooperative relationship, and not just occasional requests for help. Maintaining such a relationship is not always easy and requires constant attention.

Secondly, it will be necessary to put together the funding needed to produce the spots or broadcasts (local FM stations often charge less than others), or to seek an exemption from the ministry or agency responsible. For these reasons, radio is not used as widely as it could by communicators working with participatory approaches involving specific community groups.

The use of rural radio should also be combined with field work to ensure that communication flows in both directions: in this case, radio can either follow and support a communication initiative being undertaken at the same time, or it can be made an integral part of that initiative as a means for allowing people to express themselves.

Local press

Local press is of course not an interactive medium. But it can greatly assist the efforts of a participatory development initiative, by informing the community or targeted decision makers on the evolution of the initiative. Again, collaboration with a journalist at the beginning of the initiative may develop into a partnership, while occasionally requesting the participation of a journalist may be considered a demand of services.

Television

Television is not used the way it could mostly because of the costs involved. In some countries where it is well-developed, community television can host debates and interventions, giving them the reach that working with small specific groups cannot have. But this is seldom the case.

In other countries, there is sometimes the possibility to connect with the producer of development programs and use television to illustrate the realization of a given community initiative, thus influencing other communities to embark on such a venture. But again, this is not very common.

There is a lot of potential though to use television in a participatory way by relying on community television viewing and discussion clubs. Experiences in India and Africa have been quite successful in using that tool. But again, costs have made it unsustainable.

"Information and communication technologies" tools

The computer as a slide show projector

Portable computers now also come with batteries that can be self-sufficient for many hours. They also fit easily in a carry-all bag. With software like PowerPoint or others, it is easy to store photographs, maps, video sequences, etc. and show them to specific groups in the field or in poor communities where there is no access to electricity. Photographs taken by the community members can also be scanned and integrated into such presentations. Likewise, comparing satellite maps with community maps, or viewing the data on the availability of water, and comparing with indigenous knowledge on the issue, etc. can be powerful activities.

Using the Internet

The Internet, especially through the use of e-mail, can link together different community initiatives. This type of communication can motivate the actors in the development initiative, and enable them to get support or relevant information or to exchange ideas.

In some cases, it is feasible to produce a web page for an initiative. Again, for the actors involved in the development initiative, it contributes to breaking the sense of isolation and nurtures the motivation to act, knowing that progress on what they are doing can be known around the world. Again, this information can also be used in the context of a similar development initiative carried out elsewhere, to show what other people have been doing in a similar context.

Different media for different uses: these women are involved in community-based management of a forest. They use songs to explain and share what they are doing and why.

Identifying communication tools for different kinds of applications.

This second section discusses the identification of appropriate tools for different usages.

For our purposes, we will consider the following usages:

1. Triggering the process of participatory communication.
2. Supporting and moderating discussion groups.
3. Extending group discussion sessions.
4. Reaching other groups or participants beyond the immediate locale.
5. Supporting learning and the exchange of knowledge.
6. Helping participants communicate with each other or with a specific group.
7. Evaluating and keeping a record of activities.

Again, this list is of course not exhaustive. The main idea is that we have to identify the use we want to make of a communication tool in a given communication activity.

Triggering the process of participatory communication

The first stage in the approach to participatory development communication consists of helping to identify a problem, its causes, and deciding on actions to take to resolve it.

In this context, photography and video recordings can be very useful in helping to identify a problem. For example, in one initiative dealing with the environment, communicators first took and developed photographs of polluted sites. They then went

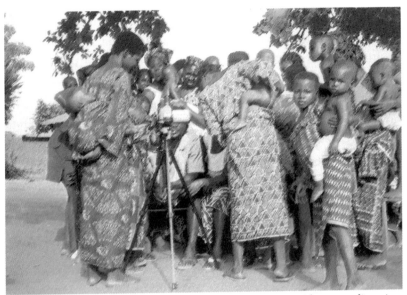

Different media for different uses: these women are preparing to video tape a discussion on the progress of their development initiative. This video recording will be shown to other groups in the community to trigger similar actions.

back to the village, showed these photographs around, and asked people what they saw in them and what they thought about them. The reactions obtained served as the basis for a subsequent discussion of the problem.

Part of the interest in using photography and video is that the equipment for producing them is affordable and easy to handle. Communicators can use these devices themselves without having to rely on help from others (audiovisual or radio specialists, theatre troupes, etc.) and participants too can easily learn to use them.

In another case, communicators distributed cameras to participants, showed them how to use them, and asked them to take pictures of problems relating to natural resource management. The photos they took were then used to conduct an in-depth discussion of those problems and of ways to resolve them.

Theatre can also be an excellent triggering tool, especially when it is combined with interactive participation by the audience (either by having individuals in the audience take the floor, or having people organize a skit themselves and present it on stage). Portraying problem situations on stage makes it possible to address sensitive issues and encourage people to express their reactions. There are amateur theatre troupes in many places, and they can often be enlisted in the process of participatory communication. Then there are comedians and professional stage directors who can come and teach participants to stage their own plays and act out the different problem situations facing them.

In some settings, much use is made of songs and sayings. Here, a *griot*, a musician or a storyteller, traditional communicators *par excellence*, can be very effective partners in the communication process. Songs can be composed for the occasion dealing with the specific topic of discussion. Or someone can be asked to tell the story of a problem that people have experienced. Some may use popular sayings or proverbs to introduce the issue. In all cases, care is required in preparing the songs, stories or sayings to be used, and tying them in with the participatory process. This approach can also be combined with audiocassette recordings, which can then be replayed in places frequented by participant groups.

Visioning sessions, involving a film or a video, can also help to pose a problem and initiate discussion on it. This requires careful preparation with the participants, so that the session does more than just convey a message, instead, it sparks real debate. Before showing the film or the video, it is important to make clear what it is about and to explain the rationale for the visioning session and the discussion that will follow.

Many NGOs, associations, local technical services, clinics and schools have films or videos dealing with various development problems. With a little local research, it should be possible to unearth materials that will serve as good triggers for discussion. The objective here is to find, not the one that provides the best coverage of the problem, but one that will help to pose the issue and evoke discussion and exchanges of view.

Similarly, it is wise to prepare a short exposé or arrange for a presentation by a resource person who could pave the way for discussion, in case the power fails or the movie projector breaks down.

A panel forum, perhaps accompanied by a presentation by a resource person, can also be useful for kicking off the process. It is important at this point to make sure that everyone has a chance to speak, and to create an atmosphere that encourages discussion, otherwise the session may turn into a question-and-answer ritual that will frustrate the attempt at participatory communication for dealing with the problem at hand.

These forums can be held in specially arranged premises, but they can also take place in spots often visited by participant groups (the marketplace, the village square, a local bar).

Discussion groups, consisting of 10 people at most, are an appropriate way of preparing a panel forum or more formal meetings with participant groups. These sessions are organized around an interview guide that the communicator has prepared in advance. Her questions are addressed to each participant in turn, and attempt to elicit information that may be useful later. The discussion group is a very practical communication tool for identifying a priority problem in the community, and its causes. It makes it possible to gather information on what participants think, and it helps in preparing a panel forum in the light of that information.

Supporting and facilitating discussion groups

Video or audio recordings of individual participants' points of view or of a group discussion may help lend depth to the debate, by allowing participants to react to what each other has said, or to go further into what they said themselves.

While video recording is more popular, audio taping with a cassette is often simpler to handle. As with radio, audio recording allows us to record and afterwards listen to discussion sessions, to share points of view and experience, and to provide useful information for subsequent discussion.

Video or audio recording of a discussion also allows the group to benefit from the viewpoints of people who can help to identify the causes of the development problem at hand (an expert on the locality or the issue), but who cannot be present at the meeting.

Videotapes can also be used to show and contrast good and bad practices, with respect to the problem identified (land use, for example), and these examples can be used to stimulate discussion and lead to decisions on concrete actions.

A video or audio recording, photographs or even posters can also be used to show examples or illustrate ideas during discussions with the participants.

An image box (flip chart) can be used to illustrate different aspects of a problem situation, and of its possible solutions, in order to spark discussion. Everything depends, however, on how it is used: the point is to show each image and ask the participants to talk about it, and then to react to each other's viewpoints.

If a theatre troupe is prepared to cooperate, we can also use theatre to illustrate different aspects of the problem or different reactions and attitudes to it, and thereby encourage thought and discussion. Here again, this may involve having a troupe perform and provoke debate with the participants, or the participants may present a skit by themselves.

Discussion groups, panel forums and visioning sessions can also be used at this stage to analyze the causes of a problem more deeply, or to decide on a solution to be implemented and tested.

Rural radio broadcasting, which leaves great room for the participants to express their points of view, can stimulate local discussion as well. It can also help to clarify the causes of a problem identified during the discussion, by bringing in resource persons and linking several elements at once. If the broadcast is recorded on a cassette, it can be used subsequently during panel forums.

Extending group discussion sessions

It can also be very useful to prolong a group session. A poster, an illustrated folder or photographs can be sent to participants after a session so that at a later time they can review or revise the information or the opinions exchanged. The participants can also use these tools to discuss the issues further with other people among their acquaintances.

These tools can be prepared separately and sent to the participants, or the participants themselves can produce them. In this case, it is important to make sure that materials (sheets of paper, pencils etc.) are available during the group discussion session for preparing these tools.

A rural radio broadcast or an article in the local paper can also be useful at this point. Here again, as is the case wherever the mass media are used, they must be incorporated into the group's work, and not simply used to convey information in one direction.

Following a discussion session, visits can be organized so that the participants can appreciate and compare initiatives undertaken by other groups, in terms of implementing an activity.

Reaching other groups or participants beyond the immediate locale

An audio or video recording of discussions with participant groups can also be used to reach out to other groups we might wish to interest in the process of participatory communication. They can also help sensitize authorities or resource persons that participants may want to enlist in the initiative supported by the communication process.

Yet again, the communicator may wish to convey the viewpoints of the participants in her own locale to the participants living in other places, in order to facilitate their participation. At this point, it is important to enlist the cooperation of a resource person to gather viewpoints and elicit discussions.

The use of rural radio should be combined with field work to ensure that communication flows in both directions: in this case, radio can either follow and support a communication initiative being undertaken at the same time, or it can be made an integral part of that initiative as a means to allow people to express themselves.

Where circumstances so permit, theatre can also fill this function. As with radio, it is important to arrange financing for the most important items (transportation, accommodation, meals etc.), and this can often pose a problem, particularly where what is involved is not a single performance but a prolonged series of presentations.

If participants want to make city dwellers or central authorities aware of the reality of rural life, we may think of using television (but more often than that, there are important costs involved). Similarly, the Internet could be useful if participants want to reach certain groups beyond the local setting, provided they are "connected". This is particularly true for NGOs, international organizations and bilateral cooperation programs, which could be approached to seek support for a development initiative. Again, in both cases, we must think of an adequate strategy to facilitate interactivity and two-way communication, and not just the dissemination of information.

Supporting learning and the exchange of knowledge

It is useful to arrange for a poster, a video or an audiotape to be accompanied by an illustrated folder or a printed text (which can be as short as one page) when we want to help participants acquire new knowledge and skills in the course of communication. This may involve learning traditional dances or songs (relating to natural resource management issues), as much as learning a new market-gardening technique or ways of managing a specific resource.

The combination of text or poster with a video or audio recording is important because the text serves to complete the image or the message: for example, it can provide guidelines for discussion, or pose questions to test comprehension, so that better use can be made of the audio or video product, or it may summarize the essential information contained in the recording. Even if most of the group is illiterate, there will generally be at least one person who can read to the others. It is important, however, to take the language factor into account when producing audio, video or printed materials.

In addition to documentation of the explanatory or demonstrative type, video recordings also make it easier to exchange knowledge between different groups of participants, such as from one village to another, by showing concrete examples and sparking discussion about the use of specific knowledge or techniques.

When conditions allow, a series of special broadcasts over rural radio, in cooperation with listeners' clubs, can be particularly useful in helping spread and exchange knowledge. When it comes to practical skills, on-the-spot demonstrations are also a good idea.

Where possible, visits to groups or individuals using this knowledge and putting it into practice can be very useful. People tend to remember best what they have seen with their own eyes. Moreover, as it generally happens during such visits, participants will ask the questions themselves, and this requires advance preparation that can often be very effective as a learning support. This requires organization and resources that are, however, not always available to everyone.

Helping participants communicate with each other or with a specific group

What are the most useful appropriate communication tools for helping the participants in the communication process to express their points of view? What tools will they feel most comfortable with, and which are best suited to the groups they are trying to reach? Which media can be used most readily and economically? The answers depend on what we are trying to achieve.

We may wish to reach other groups of participants and make them aware of the viewpoints exchanged during a discussion session. Or we may help the participants make their viewpoints known to a specific group, the local or national authorities for example, in order to sensitize them to local conditions and needs.

We may use simple tools such as video or audio recordings, or we may turn to the mass media, if funding is available to cover costs. In addition to enlisting the cooperation of the producer, participant groups can also be trained to produce their own broadcasts. The use of photographs and images can also help participants in expressing their view points. Games and group exercises are also particularly helpful in "breaking the ice" and facilitating interactions between participants.

Evaluating and keeping a record of activities

We can also use photographs, audio and video tapes to record a problem situation as it exists at the beginning of the communication process, and then compare these records with the situation at the end of the initiative. This will help us evaluate what has been accomplished.

Photos, video or tape recordings of sessions, or the simple recording of notes on a tape recorder, can also be used to document the initiative. It is important to think of this at the outset and to have a plan in mind, so that we do not find ourselves with countless hours of tape recordings or hundreds of photographs. We may want to label those recorded portions that we want to keep for documentation purposes or for building a photo album, by entering the activity and the time of production on each one.

Finally, in some cases, communicators have been able to interest journalists from the local press in covering their activities. Such articles, besides sensitizing public opinion to the initiative, have been found useful for documenting and publicizing an initiative beyond the limited group of participants. Once again, the list of tools offered here, as well as the guidelines for using them, is by no means exhaustive. Each of the teams will want to supplement the list by drawing upon examples given above to select the most appropriate communication tools.

Conclusion

Participation is the essential condition for development to happen. Development research and the implementation of development initiatives will not have much impact without the effective participation of the communities. But which kind of participation are we referring to? Are communities really getting involved in the decision-making process concerning the planning and realization of such initiatives, or are they only consulted or mobilized?

These questions also raise the degree of communication between the development practitioners or researchers and the local communities. Communication is an essential part of participatory research and development. The way the researcher or practitioner will approach a local community, the attitude she will adopt in interacting with community members, the way she will understand and discuss issues, the way she will collect and share information involve ways of establishing communication with people. The way this communication will be established and nurtured will affect the way in which people will feel involved in the issues raised and the way in which they will participate – or not participate – in a research or a development initiative.

Participatory development communication is about involving communities in development projects and development research. It is a tool, not a recipe. Communication is essential, but by itself, it is insufficient if the material, human and financial resources needed to carry out the development initiative itself, do not accompany it. Likewise, those resources are insufficient if there is no communication to facilitate community participation and appropriation of their own development.

This guide is just a starting point to the practice of participatory development communication. It has to be adapted to each context, by the main actors involved in the research or development activities. It also has to be nourished by the lessons of experience and of learning from poor communities who, through communication, take ownership by themselves for the leadership of development initiatives.

If you are interested in sharing some of these lessons, please send any comments, questions or suggestions to <gbessette@idrc.ca>.

Bibliography

Alexandre, L. & Bessette, G. (2000) *L'appui au développement communautaire, une expérience de communication en Afrique de l'ouest*. Ottawa et Paris: CRDI et Agence Intergouvernementale de la Francophonie.

Berrigan, F.J. (1981) *Community Media and Development*. Paris: UNESCO.

Bessette, G. & Rajasunderam, C.V. (Eds.) (1996) *Participatory Communication for Development: A West African Agenda*. Ottawa: IDRC and Penang: Southbound.

Casmir, F.L. (1991) *Communication in Development*. Norwood: NJ, Ablex Publishing Corporation.

Chambers, R. (1997) *Whose Reality Counts? Puttingthe First Last*. London: Intermediate Technology.

Chin, Saik Yoon (1996) 'Participatory Communication for Development'. In Bessette, G. and Rajasunderam, (Eds.) *Participatory Communication for Development: A West African Agenda*. Ottawa: IDRC and Penang: Southbound.

Coldevin, G. (2001) *Participatory Communication*. Rome: Communication for Development Group, FAO.

Dudley, E. (1993) *The Critical Villager: Beyond Community Participation*. London, New York: Routledge.

Fraser, C. & Restrepo-Estrada, S. (1998) *Communicatingfor Development: Human Change for Survival*. London, New York: I.B. Tauris.

Fraser, C. & Villet, J. (1994) *Communication: A Key to Human Development*. Rome: FAO.

Freire, P. (1970) *The Pedagogy of the Oppressed*. New York: N.Y., Continuum, 1993.

Gumucio, Dragon A. (2001) *Making Waves, Stories of Participatory Communication for Social Change: A Report to the Rockefeller Foundation.* New York: Rockefeller Foundation.

MacBride, S. (1980) *Many Voices, One World: Report of the International Study Commission on Communication Problems.* Paris: UNESCO.

Melkote, S. (1991) *Communication for Development in the Third World: Theory and Practice.* New Delhi-London: Sage Publications.

Rogers, E. (1976) *Communication and Development, Critical Perspectives.* Beverly Hills, London, Delhi: Sage Publications.

Servaes, J., Jacobson, T., White, S. (Eds.) (1996) *Participatory Communication for Social Change.* New Delhi, London: Thousand Oaks.

Servaes, J. (1999) *Communication for Development: One World, Multiple Cultures.* Creskill, NJ: Hampton Press.

White, A., Sadanandan, N.K., Ascroft, J. (Eds.) (1995) *Participatory Communication: Working for Change and Development.* New Delhi: Sage Publications.

Major trends in development communication

The experience of the past fifty years has demonstrated the crucial importance of communication in the field of development. Within the perspective of development communication, two trends developed successively: an approach that favoured large-scale actions and relied on the mass media, and an approach that promoted grassroots communication (also called community communication), promoting small-scale projects and relying especially on small media (videos, posters, slide presentation, etc.).

These trends, which still co-exist today to various degrees within the field of development communication, are linked to the evolution of the development and communication models that have marked development efforts up to now.

As a matter of fact, the first development models were defined exclusively by their economic variables. As the MacBride Commission report noted:

The former models used communication especially for disseminating information, for getting people to understand the "benefits" promised by development and the "sacrifices" it demands. The imitation of a development model, based on the hypothesis that wealth, once acquired, will automatically filter down to all levels of society, included the propagation of communication practices from top to bottom...The effects were a long way from the effects that were expected.

(MacBride 1980, p. 6)

The trend toward mass communication initially marked the first two decades during which the media were utilized in the field of development. It espoused the idea that it was enough to disseminate the knowledge and technologies of the North to ensure that they were adopted. Once adopted, they would achieve the development of the South. This first vision of development is referred to as the paradigm of "modernization".

These initial experiences, centred mainly around the mass media, relied both on a communication model based on persuasion and information transmission, and on a development model based on increasing economic activity and changes in values and attitudes.

The intervention paradigm of these two decades, which is found in two publications that had a decisive impact on the orientations adopted at that time – *The Passing of Traditional Society* by Daniel Lerner (1958) and *Mass Media and National Development* by Wilbur Schramm (1964) – consists of a very simple communication model. This can be described in stimulus-response terms, based both on the logic of persuasion and on a development model linking the latter to increased productivity.

One of the models resulting from this paradigm that had a major influence on communication practices in the area of educational development is the innovation dissemination model.

This model, resulting from an extension of agricultural practices exported to developing countries, involves the transmission of information to farmers by a resource person and was formulated in theory by Everett Rogers in 1962. This theory rested on three main elements: the target population of the innovation, the innovation to be transmitted, and the sources and communication channels.

This model has been criticized by several people for its reductionism. It did not take sufficiently into account the different types of target populations (e.g., prosperous farmers who own land and are open to new techniques versus other farmers who are illiterate, poor and exploited). It also failed to take into account the impact of the economic and political structures on the capacity to adopt innovations. The same charge of blindness where social, political and economic factors are concerned also applies to innovations that require a process of diffusion. Finally, communication channels and sources were generally used within the framework of vertical, top-down communication. There was never any mention of horizontal communication between the groups in the communities affected by the problem that the innovation was meant to resolve. There was also a lack of vertical, bottom-up communication, which would have made it possible to bring the people's problems to the attention of the decision makers and the experts.

Since then, the development and communication models have evolved considerably. The vast amount of experience in the use of the media for educational or informative purposes in the development process has led to the development of new orientations and new practices. At the same time, several criticisms have been raised with regard to the first development models and to the functionalist vision of the development communication model.

A new model emphasizing the endogenous character of development has made it possible to define development as a global process, for which societies are responsible. In this new perspective, development is not something that can come from the outside. It is a participatory process of social change within a given society (Rogers 1976, p. 133). This model has also made it possible to extend the concept of development to non-material notions by bringing into the equation notions of social equality, liberty, revenue distribution, grassroots participation in development, etc.

The conceptions everyone had of the role of communication in development have changed radically. In the first development model, the communication paradigm consisted of transmitting the technology necessary for the growth of productivity. In the second, it consists of stimulating the potential for change within a community. The concept of grassroots participation in the development process has become a key concept.

The first result of these changes in vision on day-to-day practice was the need to move from a relatively simple vision of a one-way transmission of technical information, to the promotion of bi- or multilateral systems based on grassroots participation.

At the same time as this change in communication and development models was taking place, two development paradigms were developing which helped to orient communication interventions.

On the one hand, several people were questioning the modernization model because they saw that communication did not lead to development, and observed that in fact, the countries of the South appeared to be sliding further and further into poverty, low salaries, and poor living conditions. This criticism, which was developed above all in Latin America, emphasized the link between this situation and the situation of economic dependence on the industrialized North: the development of the countries in the North was conditional on the underdevelopment of the countries of the Third World, and the "centre"developed at the expense of the "periphery".

This situation is referred to as the paradigm of "dependence". According to this paradigm, obstacles to development come first and foremost from external, not internal, obstacles: that is to say, the international economic system. Consequently, the mass media cannot act as agents of change, since they transmit the western message, and the capitalist and conservative ideology. This paradigm, which is still in existence today, was also criticized because it put too much emphasis on the contradictions at the international level and not enough on the contradictions at the local and national levels. The resulting discussions and recommendations regarding the "new information order" related to this paradigm.

Its extension at the national level emphasized the relationship between communication and politicization. One of the models resulting from this paradigm, which exercised in the past, and today still exercises a determining influence on the development communication practices, is the consciousness model developed by Paolo Freire (1973). Freire, and several other communicators after him, identified communication as a process that is inseparable from the social and political processes necessary for development.

Freire insisted on the fact that the mere transfer of knowledge by an authority source to a passive receiver did nothing to help promote growth in the latter as a human being with an independent and critical conscience capable of influencing and changing society. According to him, for development communication to be effective, it had to be linked not only to the process of acquiring technical knowledge and skills, but also to the awareness-raising, politicization and organization processes.

In his model, which he explains in *The Pedagogy of the Oppressed* (Freire 1973), development communication can be considered as a tool that the grassroots can use to take control. This tool can be used for the following purposes: becoming aware of the various facets of the real development problems in their region; organizing in order to react collectively and effectively to these problems; bringing to light the conflicts that divide the various interest groups; becoming politicized – learning to provide alternatives to problem situations and finding solutions to various problems; and obtaining the necessary tools to put to concrete use the solutions provided by the community.

This model and its applications have also been subject to criticism. It was stated, among other things, that politicization through the community media may constitute an adequate approach in countries that tolerate recourse to political action; but in most developing countries, this political action would lead to the overthrow of the governing, "have" elite without providing the means for changing conditions, and the confrontations that follow would commonly lead to repression and regression of democratic rights (on this point, see Berrigan 1981, p. 41).

Thus, rather than a direct politicization approach, many prefer an approach based on education, where the objective is not to cause a confrontation but to provide the tools necessary for organization.

A third paradigm orienting the formulation of development communication models and interventions is one that is generally called "the paradigm of another development". This paradigm emphasizes not only material development but also the development of values and cultures. Where development communication interventions are concerned, it emphasizes the small media operating in networks and the use of grassroots communication approaches. According to this paradigm, grassroots participation reinforces the chances that communities will adopt activities appropriate for them.

One of the models attached to this paradigm is the methodology of community media.

"Wherever carefully developed programs have failed", states a UNESCO study, "this approach, which consists in helping people to formulate their problems or to acquire an awareness of new options, instead of imposing on them a plan that was formulated elsewhere, makes it possible to intervene more effectively in the real space of the individual or the group" (Berrigan 1981, p. 13).

The concept of interactivity, with the small media as its operational instrument, makes possible the endogenous acquisition of knowledge and skills within the framework of a search for solutions and the communication process. This is referred to as a recourse to a methodology of community media, whose principal elements are:

- identification of needs by means of direct contacts with the groups;
- concretization: examination of the problem identified by the groups in the light of local conditions;
- selection of priority problems by the groups;
- formulation of a durable methodology for seeking solutions;
- identification of the amount of information required and access to this information;
- action: execution by the groups of the projects they have designed;
- expansion toward the outside to make known the points of view of the groups to other groups or to the authorities;
- liaison with the communication system to make known their action (Berrigan 1981).

Other models combine different concepts. This is true, for example, of the practices for supporting communication in development projects, which combined the community approach and recourse to the small media with practices that can often be linked to a model for disseminating the innovations.

This approach emphasizes the planning of communication activities as a support to a development project. Its aim is to produce a common understanding or a consensus among all the participants in a development initiative. It emphasizes the facilitation of exchanges of points of view among the various people involved and aims at taking into account the grassroots perceptions in the planning of the project and mobilizing them in the development activities set out in the project. The methodology results from educational technology and is characterized by the integration of needs analysis and evaluation mechanisms in the communication process.

Other practices are based on the community approach and the grassroots awareness-raising model. The same is true of the alternative for democratic development communication, which emphasizes grassroots access to the communication process for the purpose of promoting social justice and democracy. In certain cases, this is translated by an emphasis on participation by the most disadvantaged in the communication process (access to small media at the local level), and in other cases, by actions promoting cultural expression and the search for ways of taking control of the mass media.

Finally, we saw recently, notably in the case of the fight against AIDS, approaches resulting from social marketing, having recourse at the same time to research techniques adapted to small groups, and to communities and the large-scale use of the mass media. We are also witnessing numerous projects utilizing new technologies and the internet as a way to support group advocacy, reinforce the circulation of information and supporting community radio and television. To these approaches we must also add numerous practices related to basic education, informal education, distance learning, literacy, and post-literacy activities that have their own methodologies, community media approaches and extension approaches.

In short, the field of development communication is vast and its divisions are numerous. The different paradigms that have marked its evolution are still active to various degrees, and the models that are attached to them are as different as their ideologies and the orientations that inspired them.

In spite of the diversity of approaches and orientations, however, there is a consensus today on the need for grassroots participation in development and on the essential role that communication plays in promoting development. This is very well said in a popular FAO slogan: "There is no development without communication" (Balit 1988).

The development communication experience over the past 40 years has taught us a lot about the role of communication in development. The main lesson probably has been the recognition of the need to move from communication practices based on the one-and-only model of information transmission removed from the community processes, to practices involving the grassroots in their development.

Our experience shows that the point of departure for development communication is not the dissemination of an innovation or of a new idea that is full of promise, but the grassroots expression of its needs. Participation, by putting the emphasis on the needs and the viewpoints of the individuals and groups, becomes the key concept of development communication. Recourse to a systemic methodology and the implementation of horizontal processes in which people are directly associated with the communication process and are thus more likely to formulate their problems themselves, become aware of new possibilities, and take their knowledge and their viewpoints into consideration in the communication process – constitute the major elements of its methodology.